Henry James &
the Art of Power

Henry James &
the Art of Power

by Mark Seltzer

Cornell University Press

Ithaca and London

This book has been published with the aid of a grant from
the Hull Memorial Publication Fund of Cornell University.

First published 1984 by Cornell University Press.
Published in the United Kingdom by Cornell University Press
Ltd., London.

International Standard Book Number 0–8014–1701–5
Library of Congress Catalog Card Number 84–7740

Printed in the United States of America

*Librarians: Library of Congress cataloging information
appears on the last page of the book.*

*The paper in this book is acid-free and meets the guidelines
for permanence and durability of the Committee on Production
Guidelines for Book Longevity of the Council on Library Resources.*

Library of Congress Cataloging in Publication Data
SELTZER, MARK, 1951–
    Henry James and the art of power.

    Includes index.
    1. James, Henry, 1843–1916—Criticism and
interpretation. 2. Power (Social sciences) in
literature. I. Title.
PS2127.P63S44 1984   813'.4   84-7740
ISBN 0-8014-1701-5 (alk. paper)

For my parents

Contents

Acknowledgments

It is a pleasure to thank the teachers and friends who have contributed, directly and indirectly, to this project: Eric Sundquist, Martin Jay, Jonathan Crewe, Carolyn Porter, Norman Grabo, Stephen Greenblatt, and Richard Bridgman; and, more recently, Cynthia Chase, Fredric Bogel, Jonathan Culler, Mary Ann Radzinowicz, and especially Laura Brown and Walter Cohen.

Walter Benn Michaels contributed to this book from its inception. I am deeply indebted to him for his generous instruction and continuing advice and friendship. The book could not have been written without the critical generosity and support of Shirley Samuels, my closest reader, best friend, and much more.

Chapter 1, in a slightly different version, appeared in *Nineteenth-Century Fiction*, vol. 35, no. 4 (1981), pp. 506–534, © 1981 by The Regents of the University of California. It is reprinted here by permission of The Regents. A version of the Postscript appeared in *Diacritics*, vol. 14, no. 1 (1984) and is reprinted here by permission of the editors.

MARK SELTZER

Ithaca, New York

Henry James &
the Art of Power

Introduction

The intent of this book is to revise the traditional view of the "politics of the novel" by way of a reading of a novelist who, we are told, was never tempted by the political and always resisted the exercise of power.[1] Not merely has Henry James been read as the very exemplar of a novelist outside the circuit of power, but further, his novelistic and critical practice has been appropriated to support an absolute opposition between aesthetic and political claims. It is this opposition between the art of the novel and the subject of power that I want to reexamine. Questioning the traditional assumption that James is essentially a nonpolitical novelist, I explore the ways in which James represents social movements of appropriation, supervision, and regulation, and examine how both the content and the techniques of representation in James's works express a complicity and rigorous continuity with the larger social regimes of mastery and control that traverse these works. I want to suggest that art and power are not opposed in the Jamesian text but radically entangled. There

---

1. See, for instance, Irving Howe's assessment of James in *Politics and the Novel* (New York: Horizon, 1957). "The temptation of politics," Howe argues, "seems never to have troubled him at all" (p. 139).

is, to adapt James's phrase, a "criminal continuity" between the techniques of representation that the novelist devises and the technologies of power that his fiction ostensibly censors and disavows.[2] Put as simply as possible, the art of the novel is an art of power.

Criticism of James has always been Jamesian, and this is the case not merely because James, in his own criticism and especially in his prefaces to the New York Edition, has so comprehensively set the terms for his own evaluation but also because Anglo-American criticism of the novel, from Percy Lubbock's *Craft of Fiction* to Wayne Booth's *Rhetoric of Fiction* and beyond, has proceeded along the lines that James has so clearly drawn. A technical and formalist emphasis has dominated Jamesian criticism, and problems of social reference have characteristically been converted into problems of textual self-reference. Thus, two of James's most perceptive readers, Richard Poirier and Laurence Holland, have concentrated on the "analogues" between James's fictional and critical practice, on, as Poirier suggests, the "problematic relationship of his most important novels to the larger questions of form . . . addressed in the Prefaces."[3]

The link has been established between the "lives enacted in the fiction" and the "central terminologies of James's criticisms."[4] One can scarcely overestimate the rich contributions of this inward commentary on the "marriage" of subject and technique in James's fiction. But one consequence of this emphasis is that even where social institutions of power and authority are invoked, they can be perceived only as an external threat to the internal balance and organic unity of the novel. In general terms, power is perceived as a threat to the "literariness" of the literary text.

There is always something scandalous about power in James's

---

2. The phrase is adapted from Henry James, *The American Scene* (Bloomington: Indiana University Press, 1968), 465.

3. Richard Poirier, Foreword to Laurence B. Holland, *The Expense of Vision: Essays on the Craft of Henry James* (Baltimore: Johns Hopkins University Press, 1982), vii.

4. Ibid.

fiction, and perhaps in the novel generally, and this criticism, following James's lead, has operated to free the novelist from what might be called *the shame of power*. The Jamesian text, it is argued, resists the impositions of power in the name of a radical (literary) freedom. The question that James always seems to be asking, as Poirier, for instance, observes, is: "Am I guilty . . . of violating the dramatic freedom of this character in order to place him in some system of meaning?"[5] More recently, another of James's best critics, Leo Bersani, has repeated and extended this claim and has clarified the recalcitrant opposition between aesthetic freedom and the systems of power and order that ground it. "The recurrent Jamesian subject," Bersani accurately argues, "is only superficially the international theme, or the confrontation of innocence and experience, or the conflict of acquisitive and self-renouncing impulses. His subject is freedom— but we must understand that word in the sense of inventions so coercive that they resist any attempt to enrich—or reduce— them with meaning."[6] From this point of view, the imposition of meaning threatens the freedom of signification, or even freedom from signification, that here characterizes the literary. For Bersani, the "coercive" inventiveness of the literary is defined precisely by its resistance to coercion, its resistance to the impositions of meaning and the impositions of power both.

But it is just this antinomy of the literary and the political that I want to question. To the extent that James's fiction is centrally concerned with freedom, its concern is also with all that is seen to constrict freedom—with law, power, and authority. Moreover, if James's texts explicitly disown the exercise of power, the discourse of his fiction is a double discourse that at once represses and acknowledges a discreet continuity between literary and political practices. Power and authority are not external interventions in the novel but are already immanent in the nov-

5. Richard Poirier, *The Comic Sense of Henry James* (New York: Oxford University Press, 1967), 9.
6. Leo Bersani, "The Jamesian Lie," in *A Future for Astyanax* (Boston: Little, Brown, 1976), 132 (chap. 5).

elist's policies of representation. In fact, the techniques of representation that James invents to defer, dissimulate, and disavow the technologies of power that pressure his texts reinvent these very technologies. And I want to argue that the Jamesian aesthetic is elaborated precisely as a way of dissimulating and disavowing the immanence of power in the novel.

I mean to suggest that James's art of representation always also involves a politics of representation, and one reason for suspecting this link between art and power is that James works so carefully to deny it. James's most familiar injunction to critics, for instance, betrays a curious inconsequence: "We must," he asserts in "The Art of Fiction," "grant the writer his subject, his idea, his donnée: our criticism is applied only to what he makes of it." The writer, he continues, must be "granted his starting point," and this referential point of departure must then be taken for granted; criticism must be reoriented from the "subject" represented to the novelist's techniques of representation. What is curious about this statement is the radical break between subject and technique that James proposes, and it is in fact just this break that James, later in the same essay, emphatically refuses. If he has seemingly restricted criticism to treatment, if his comments have perhaps implied that a "novel should be all treatment and no subject," James goes on to insist that the "idea, the starting point . . ., permeates and penetrates" the novel and, further, that it is just this notion of the "idea and the form" as being even provisionally separated and "known apart" that illegitimately allows for the novel to be "spoken of as something different from its organic whole."[7]

The contradiction that troubles James's account of the subject of fiction is clear enough. But for the moment I am concerned less with the local contradiction that James's essay displays than with the more general anxiety that leads James to risk this contradiction. James, in "The Art of Fiction," is of course arguing

---

7. Henry James, "The Art of Fiction," in *Partial Portraits* (1888; reprint ed., New York: Haskell House, 1968), 394–95, 400.

against a criticism that would prescribe "proper" subjects for the novel. More specifically, he is responding to the naturalist's emphasis, Zola's in particular, on the fidelity to the "given," to the novel's "starting point" and referential point of origin. For the naturalist writer, the novel's referential *point d'appui* determines—indeed predetermines—the consequent movement of the novel. As Zola observes in "The Experimental Novel," "we begin certainly with true facts which are our indestructible base." The novel begins with the "true facts" of nature and proceeds "without departing from nature." The naturalist's point of departure confines his practice, a confinement ruled over by what Zola calls the "fixed laws" of fact. Indeed, this appeal to the law is central to Zola's project. The experimental novelist seeks "knowledge of the laws" of society, and this access to knowledge is also an access to power. The dream of the novelist is to master the law, "to be master of good and evil, to regulate life, to regulate society . . . , above all to bring a solid foundation to justice by experimentally resolving questions of criminality." The determinism of the naturalist novelist ultimately represents a policing action.[8]

It is in part his attempt to displace this "legal" scenario that moves James to hold out for a free grant of the novel's donnée and to open up a contradictory space between subject or starting point and treatment. James in "The Art of Fiction" is finally arguing against a criticism that would dictate "lawful" subjects for the novel, making it "lawful to touch one and unlawful to touch another." The presumption that "laws of fiction may be laid down," James everywhere insists, limits the absolute "liberty of interpretation" that makes the novel, as a form, "perfectly free."[9] I will be addressing the politics of naturalism and realism in detail in the following chapters, the way in which the novel enforces a certain legality in its very forms and techniques of

8. Emile Zola, "The Experimental Novel," in *Documents of Modern Literary Realism*, ed. George J. Becker (Princeton: Princeton University Press, 1963), 168, 171, 177.
9. Henry James, "The Art of Fiction," 386, 398–99.

representation. What must be emphasized here is that James's art of fiction is formulated precisely in response to the pressures of the law, in both a literary and political sense. And his attempt to keep the novel free and outside the law here betrays James into contradiction.

The Jamesian resistance to the law in the name of an absolute novelistic liberty, however, in fact works as a "cover" for a discreet and comprehensive entanglement between strategies of representation and exercises of power and law in the Jamesian text. The law does not invade James's fiction from the outside; it is already inscribed in James's novelistic practice. James's fiction, and indeed the late nineteenth-century novel in general, proclaims its outlawry even as the novel reproduces and promotes social systems of legality, supervision, and regulation. The novel secures and extends the very movements of power it ostensibly abjures. And the double discourse by which power is at once exercised and screened registers, as we will see, the discretion achieved by modern technologies of social control, a discretion that allows for the dissemination of power throughout the most everyday social practices and institutions, including the institution of the novel itself.

The readings that follow attempt to define these social networks of power and the ways in which the novel invokes and underwrites them. In the first chapter, centered on *The Princess Casamassima,* I consider how the Jamesian techniques of narrative seeing and point of view reproduce social modes of surveillance and supervision, and moreover how the realist project operates through a comprehensive surveillance and policing of the real. James, in his later fiction, rejects this too-evident narrative policing and elaborates a more tactful and more comprehensive style of supervision. Hence in the next chapter, focused on *The Golden Bowl,* I explore the manner in which the imperative of organic form guarantees the Jamesian values of love and freedom even as it achieves a virtually "automatic" regulation of character and narrative. The revision of narrative style, I try to show, participates in a more general shift in social policies of control. I then investigate James's representation of America in *The American Scene*, a text that provides James's most extensive account of the links between forms of discourse and the structures of power.

In the final two chapters, I consider the politics in and of the novel from a somewhat different perspective. In part, I address the ways in which recent theories of an intrinsic literary "difference" ultimately underwrite the very strategies of power these theories are imagined to subvert; more generally, I take up these matters by way of the recent histories of social practices of discipline and regulation provided by Michel Foucault, whose analytics of the entanglements between power and discourse lie at the back of my study throughout. Clearly, I have not attempted a wall-to-wall analysis of James's work. Rather, I have chosen to focus on these texts because they seem to me to exemplify most fully James's treatment of the subject of power and the mutations in that treatment, mutations in the style of power. James's texts achieve what might be called an aesthetic rewriting of power, and at every point I will be concerned with what this rewriting can tell us about the politics of the novel generally. My analyses extend beyond James to a consideration of the ways in which the novel, as a form and as an institution, reinscribes and supplements social mechanisms of policing and regulation.

I have indicated in a general and preliminary way the terms of my project. My method throughout, however, is to situate James's texts historically, and it is necessary to indicate how I am conceiving the "historicity" of the novel. Recent literary theory has been dominated by two apparently antithetical views of history. A convenient way of locating these alternative views is by contrasting James's representation of the basis of historical knowledge in his most explicitly "political novel," *The Princess Casamassima*, to Zola's rather different account in *Germinal*, published in 1885, the same year that James's novel was beginning to appear serially. Viewing the cultural monuments in Paris and Venice, Hyacinth Robinson shifts his allegiance from political and revolutionary to cultural and aesthetic commitments, and he writes to the Princess to inform her of this shift, to tell her *"le fond de ma pensée."* But Hyacinth in fact makes reference to several not entirely compatible "bases" of his thought and social bottom lines. At one extreme, Hyacinth recognizes that "the monuments and treasures of art . . . , the general fabric of civilization, as we know it, [are] based if you will upon all the despotisms, the cruelties, the exclusions, the monopolies and the rapacities of the past"; but at the other extreme, this foundation of exploitation competes with a radically different version of the base of social action, "that kind of invidious jealousy which is at the bottom of the idea of a redistribution."[10]

Now, the multiple and contradictory accounts of the base of society implicitly invoke one of the founding assumptions of the realist project itself. The "lower elements" in the realist text function both as a model of society (the pursuit of the real involves the uncovering of the under classes) and as a model of truth (the real lies hidden and beneath). *The Princess Casamassima* displays the interdependency of these two models. The Princess associates "reality" and the "real London" with the lower classes, and the "gathering force underground" constitutes political reality, "the mystery beneath the surface . . . nothing of it appears above the surface."[11] But we can scarcely equate the Princess's notion of the real with James's own, and the competition of bases that James represents effectively undoes this epistemological and social base of reference, defers and displaces the premises of realism.

Zola's *Germinal,* on the contrary, exploits a blunt convergence of these models of the real. The climactic explosion of the mine at Le Voreux constitutes what might be called the realist moment in Zola's novel, fusing literal and figurative readings of political action. The rising up of the lower classes—the "germination" that will "crack the earth asunder"—is literalized in the upheaval of what has been hidden beneath the surface. The

---

10. Henry James, *The Princess Casamassima* (New York: Scribner's, 1908), 2:145–46.
11. Ibid., 1:221, 2:48–49.

explosion explicitly stands (in) for "that day when the last expiring bourgeois [will] hear the very stones of the streets exploding under their feet." The social base, which is also for Zola the indestructible base of historical truth, the gathering reality underground, could not be more impressively or univocally enacted.[12]

I will be returning to James's treatment of the political underground and to his staging and resituating of these realist assumptions. For the moment it may be noted that these two accounts of the social base—the proliferation and displacement of bottoms in *The Princess Casamassima*, the literalizing of an underground repository of the real in *Germinal*—strikingly correspond to two governing positions in contemporary literary theory that have generally been seen to be absolutely opposed. I am referring to the accounts of literary history articulated in deconstructive and Marxist criticism and more particularly in the versions offered by the leading American exponents of these two theoretical positions, Paul de Man and Fredric Jameson.

De Man, in his essay "Literary History and Literary Modernity," attempts to "revise the foundations of literary history." This revision of foundations centrally involves an equation of "literary interpretation" and "literary history," the refusal in fact of any ground or base of literary history. "[T]he bases for historical knowledge," de Man asserts, "are not empirical facts but written texts, even if these texts masquerade in the guise of wars or revolutions."[13] This claim of course points to a basis of historical knowledge even as the very notion of a foundation or base is debased or even elided. The textualizing of history means that history is simply one form of interpretation—or rather misinterpretation—among others. More recently, de Man has elaborated on the view of fiction entailed by this displacement of the ground of historical knowledge. Not merely is history invalidated as the referential base of the literary text, but moreover,

12. Emile Zola, *Germinal* (New York: Penguin, 1954), 449, 453.

13. Paul de Man, *Blindness and Insight* (New York: Oxford University Press, 1971), 165.

the notion of referentiality itself is seen to violate the pure literariness of the literary text. "Fiction has nothing to do with representation," de Man insists, "but is the absence of any link between utterance and a referent." Despite the "illusion" of reference in the novel, the language of fiction is actually "entirely free with regard to referential meaning." De Man thus theorizes the literary freedom that James appeals to in "The Art of Fiction" and that Poirier and Bersani, as we have seen, reiterate. The literary moment is that moment when "the fiction stands free of any signification," and this is a freedom from both meaning and history.[14]

The Marxist critic's view of the basis of literary history is of course very different. For Fredric Jameson, for example, the literary text may "repress" its historicity, but the "ground base of material production continues underneath the new formal structures" of the novel. History grounds the literary text, and this history beneath the surface must be uncovered and disclosed. The problem here, however, is that history for Jameson is both "a ground and . . . an absent cause." That is, for Jameson history is always "History," the absent referent or hidden God, the "ultimate ground" of the literary discourse, but a ground that always escapes detection. Jameson speaks of the "path of the object" and the "path of the subject" but maintains that these paths never really cross. Neither history nor the text is ever confronted "in all its freshness as a thing-in-itself," and thus the "Marxist ideal of understanding" remains ideal or illusory. Although interpretive strategies may project the "illusion that their readings are somehow complete and self-sufficient," any reading for Jameson—as for de Man—is necessarily "a misreading."[15]

If for de Man the scandal of fiction is its freedom from reference, for Jameson the scandal appears in an appeal to a referen-

14. Paul de Man, "The Purloined Ribbon," *Glyph 1: Johns Hopkins Textual Studies* (Baltimore: Johns Hopkins University Press, 1977), 39, 40.

15. Fredric Jameson, *The Political Unconscious* (Ithaca: Cornell University Press, 1981), 215, 101, 9, 10, 266.

tial ground that is always absent. But whether this nonreferentiality is conceived as a form of freedom or a form of loss, these two very different attitudes toward literary history are linked by an account of the grounds of interpretation that is fundamentally mistaken and mistaken in a way that undermines both theoretical projects. For the deconstructionist, the fiction-in-itself is never readable, for to read is to impose a "falsely referential" meaning on the freestanding text; for the Marxist, the "things in themselves" are never knowable, because reading subjects always impose "the concepts and categories by which we attempt to understand those things."[16] But these problems only arise if one remains attached to an ideal reading or meaning that lies somehow beneath or outside the impositions of interpretation. These accounts of meaning ultimately insist, as Walter Benn Michaels has shown, "on an idealized (impossible) account of the true"; they insist on an ideal of objectivity or disinterestedness, and "it is only when measured against this disinterested ideal that all (inevitably interested) readings can be appropriately called misreadings."[17] These accounts of literary history at once acknowledge and work to repress, then, precisely those interests, enforcements, and impositions that constitute what counts as true. What de Man ultimately wants to free the literary text from, and what Jameson's argument for "the priority of the political interpretation of literary texts" paradoxically wants to escape, is thus the inevitable politics of interpretation.[18] These theories, from opposite sides, attempt to free the text from the movements of interest, power, and desire through a movement of idealization that displays above all a fear of power. One might even say that every attempt to theorize the base of historical knowledge—every attempt to ground interpretation outside or beneath the risks of practice—is motivated by such a fear, by a desire to disavow the crime of power.

---

16. Ibid., 9.
17. Walter Benn Michaels, "Saving the Text: Reference and Belief," *MLN* 93 (1978), 789–90.
18. Jameson, *The Political Unconscious*, 17.

Hence I am interested not so much in a theory of power as in the politics of theory. If, as Michel Foucault has claimed, "interpretation is the violent or surreptitious appropriation of a system of rules . . . in order to impose a direction, to bend it to a new will, to force its participation in a different game," then what I want is radically to redirect the traditional course of Jamesian criticism, to expose the ruses that have maintained an opposition between the art of the novel and the subject of power, to change the rules by which we speak of the politics of the novel.[19] It is the criminal continuity between art and power and the ways in which the novelist and critic—through an aesthetic and theoretical rewriting of power—have worked to disown it that I want to examine. The novel does not simply refer to an "extraliterary" history or politics that lies beyond it; nor is history merely a ground or background of the literary text. The movements of power do not lie in some hidden depths, but are visible on the surfaces of the literary discourse; and the historicity of the text is to be sought not in the grand designs and teleology of an absent History but in the microhistories and micropolitics of the body and the social body, in the minute and everyday practices and techniques that the novel registers and secures. What follows is an attempt to define these practices and techniques and to trace the immanence of power in the novel.

19. Michel Foucault, "Nietzsche, Genealogy, History," in *Language, Counter-Memory, Practice* (Ithaca: Cornell University Press, 1977), 151–52.

1

The Princess Casamassima: Realism and the Fantasy of Surveillance

I

"We do not suffer from the spy mania here," George R. Sims observes in his monograph on the London underworld, *The Mysteries of Modern London;* in this "free land," he argues, it is "not our custom to take violent measures" against the secret agents of the nether world. The freedom from violence that Sims celebrates, however, carries a rider that he at once suggests and disavows, and the "spy mania" reappears in a somewhat different guise: "The system of observation is as perfect as can be. . . . every foreign anarchist and terrorist known to the police—and I doubt if there is one in our midst who is not—is shadowed." London's "freedom" is guaranteed by the existence of an unlimited policing and by the dissemination of elaborate methods of police surveillance. An intense watchfulness generalizes the spy mania that Sims has discounted, and for the violence of the law is substituted a more subtle and more extensive mode of power and coercion: a power of observation and surveillance, and a seeing that operates as a more effective means of overseeing. Nor is it merely, in Sims's account, the agents of secret societies and criminals of the underworld who are shadowed by this perfect system of observation. London itself is constituted as a secret society, and everyday life is riddled with suggestions of criminality and encompassed by an incriminating surveillance:

> In the 'buses and the trams and the trains the silent passengers sit side by side, and no man troubles about his neighbour. But the mysteries of modern London are represented in the crowded vehicle and in the packed compartment. The quiet-looking woman sitting opposite you in the omnibus knows the secret that the police have been seeking to discover for months. The man who politely raises his hat because he touches you as he passes from his seat would, if the truth were known, be standing in the dock of the Old Bailey to answer a capital charge.

The melodrama of the secret crime and the secret life passes "side by side with all that is ordinary and humdrum in the monotony of everyday existence." And since there are "no mysteries of modern London more terrible than its unrecorded ones," "silence" can only imply a more nefarious criminality; and not to have been brought to book by the police can only invoke a suspicion of mysteries more insidious and of a criminality more threatening in its apparent innocence and ordinariness.[1]

If Sims's vision of the London streets is marked by a fantastic paranoia, it is also a remarkable piece of police work, an attempt to "book" London's unrecorded mysteries and to supplement the official police record through an unrestricted lay policing. Discovering mysteries everywhere, Sims places all of London under suspicion and under surveillance. Nor is Sims's vision untypical of the manner in which London is seen and recorded in the late nineteenth century. The extensive documentation that accumulates about London from the mid-century on displays an interesting paradox. On the one hand, from George W. M. Reynolds's *The Mysteries of London* (1845–1848) to Sims's *The*

---

1. George R. Sims, *The Mysteries of London* (London: C. Arthur Pearson, 1906), 81, 10, 8.

Mysteries of Modern London (1906), London was reproduced as an impenetrable region of mystery; on the other, as this proliferating literature itself testifies, London was subjected to an unprecedented and elaborate scrutiny and surveillance. The sense of the city as an area of mystery incites an intensive policing, a police work not confined to the institutions of the law (although the expansion of the London police and detective forces was "a landmark in the history of administration")[2] but enacted also through an "unofficial" literature of detection: by the reports of tourists from the "upper world" and by the investigations of an exploratory urban sociology, particularly the work of Henry Mayhew, Charles Booth, and B. Seebohm Rowntree. It is played out also in the "discovery" of the city, and its underworld, by the realist and naturalist novelists.

Henry James's eccentric contribution to the literature of London exploration is *The Princess Casamassima*, his vision of the "sinister anarchic underworld" of London. "Truly, of course," James observes in his preface to the novel, "there are London mysteries (dense categories of dark arcana) for every spectator." *The Princess Casamassima* is a novel about the mysteries of London, about spies and secret societies, and it is also a novel about spectatorship, about seeing and being seen. James offers an obligingly simple account of the novel's origin: "This fiction proceeded quite directly, during the first year of a long residence in London, from the habit and the interest of walking the streets." "The attentive exploration of London," he suggests, ". . . fully explains a large part" of the novel; one walked "with one's eyes greatly open," and this intense observation provoked "a mystic solicitation, the urgent appeal, on the part of everything, to be interpreted."[3] It is the insistent continuity between

---

2. Francis Sheppard, *London, 1808–1870: The Infernal Wen* (Berkeley: University of California Press, 1971), 36.

3. Henry James, *The Princess Casamassima* (New York: Scribner's, 1908), 1:xxi, vii, v. Subsequent references to the novel and to the preface are to this edition (vols. 5 and 6 of the New York Edition) and appear in parentheses in the text.

secrecy and spectatorship, between the "mysteries abysmal" of London and the urgent solicitation to interpretation, that I want to focus on in this study of *The Princess Casamassima.* More precisely, I want to explore two questions that this continuity poses. First, what does it mean to walk the streets of London at this time, and how does this street walking function as a metonymy for the ways in which London is seen by James and his contemporaries? Second, how do the content and the techniques of representation in James's novel reproduce the London spy mania and the coercive network of seeing and power that characterize the literature of London mysteries?

Critics of *The Princess Casamassima* have traditionally located its politics in James's representation of London anarchist activities and have largely dismissed the novel's political dimension by pointing to James's lack of knowledge about these activities. The critical impulse has been to rescue the significance of the text by redirecting attention away from its ostensible political subject to its techniques, and these techniques have been seen to be at odds with the novel's political references. Manfred Mackenzie has recently summarized this depoliticization of the text, claiming that James, "because of his prior or primary American association . . . , cannot participate in any conventional modes of European social power, only in 'seeing,' or 'knowledge,' or 'consciousness.' "[4]

But can "seeing" and "power" be so easily opposed in this literature, and are the politics of *The Princess Casamassima* separable from its techniques, from its ways of seeing and ways of knowing? What I hope to demonstrate is that *The Princess Casamassima* is a distinctly political novel but that James's analysis

---

4. Manfred Mackenzie, *Communities of Honor and Love in Henry James* (Cambridge: Harvard University Press, 1976), 3. See also Lionel Trilling, *The Liberal Imagination* (New York: Viking, 1950), 92; Irving Howe, *Politics and the Novel* (Cleveland: Meridian Books, 1957), 146; John Goode, "The Art of Fiction: Walter Besant and Henry James," in *Tradition and Tolerance in Nineteenth-Century Fiction,* ed. David Howard, John Lucas, and John Goode (London: Routledge, 1966), 280; and Lyall H. Powers, *Henry James and the Naturalist Movement* (East Lansing: Michigan State University Press, 1971), 119.

of anarchist politics is less significant than the power play that the narrative technique itself enacts. This is not to say that the politics of the novel are confined to its techniques: the institutions of the law and its auxiliaries, primarily the prison and the police, function as explicit topics in the text. But beyond these explicit and local representations of policing power, there is a more discreet kind of policing that the novel engages, a police work articulated precisely along the novel's line of sight.

II

If a relation between seeing and power becomes evident in the literature of the London underworld, it asserts itself not because the writer acknowledges the relation but, rather, because he works so carefully to disavow it. Sims, for instance, denies the existence of a "spy mania" on two counts: first, by separating police surveillance from an exercise of power, and second, by attempting to draw a line between his own acts of espionage and those of the police. Sims insists that he does not require a police escort in his wanderings through the London streets: "I have never asked for their assistance in my journeyings into dark places."[5] Nevertheless, he is uneasily aware of the incriminating cast of his prowling and publication of the London netherworld. In his earlier *How the Poor Live and Horrible London* (1883), he notes that "it is unpleasant to be mistaken, in underground cellars where the vilest outcasts hide from the light of day, for detectives in search of their prey."[6] Techniques of "disinterested" information gathering are unpleasantly mistaken for exercises of social control.

Additionally, Sims attempts to defend himself from another kind of "mistake," a misreading that would similarly put his

5. Sims, *The Mysteries of Modern London*, 12.
6. Cited in Jack Lindsay, Introduction to Jack London, *The People of the Abyss* (1903; reprint of 1st ed., London: Journeyman Press, 1977), 7.

motives in question. He introduces his text with a series of dis-
claimers: "It is not my object in these pages to bring out the
sensational features of police romance"; my task "has for its
object not the gratifying of a morbid curiosity, but the better
understanding of things as they are." But if Sims seeks to tell
"only the truth . . . , a plain unvarnished tale," his account,
again, everywhere takes the form of what he protests against. If
he will reveal only the truth, it is because the "truth is stranger
than any written tale could ever hope to be"; and he proceeds to
detail the underworld of East London as "the romances of the
'Mysterious East.' "[7] His motives and, by implication, the motives
of his audience cannot be separated from a morbid curiosity-
mongering.

Sims's works sensationalize the mysteries beneath the humdrum surface and posit lurid secrets to be detected; they incite
and cultivate a fascination with the underworld that converts it
into a bizarre species of entertainment. On the one side, putting
the underworld into discourse takes the form of a certain detective work, on the other, the purveying of a sensational entertainment. It is between these two poles—policing and entertainment—that Sims wishes to situate his texts, disclaiming both his
(mis)identification as a detective and his exploitation of an intru-
sive voyeurism. Sims tries to open up a narrow space—called
"things as they are"—to evade the charge of violating what he
sees and reports. But this space is eroded from both sides:
watching cannot be freed from an act of violation, from a conversion of the objects of his investigation into, as he expresses it,
the "victims of my curiosity."[8]

The double bind in which Sims finds himself, and the alibis he
offers to extricate himself, recur frequently in other representations of the London underworld. This literature is always, in
effect, playing on the twin senses of "bringing to book," making
it difficult to disentangle publication from incrimination, and

---

7. Sims, *The Mysteries of Modern London*, 9–14.
8. Ibid., 12.

foregrounding the police work always latent in the retailing of London mysteries. James Greenwood, in his *Low-Life Deeps: An Account of the Strange Fish to be Found There* (1881), feels compelled, like Sims, to offer apologies for his intrusions into the underworld: "The extraordinary endurance of popular interest in the 'Orton imposture' . . . will perhaps be regarded as sufficient justification for here reproducing what was perhaps the most conclusive evidence of the man's guilt at the time, or since brought to light." Greenwood, however, does more than reproduce the evidence and respond, after the fact, to popular demand. His own investigations have in fact produced the confession and its accompanying popularity. Greenwood has brought Orton to book in the double sense that I have indicated: "I am glad to acknowledge that the confession of 'brother Charles' was obtained by me, the more so when I reflect on the vast amount of patience and perseverance it was found necessary to exercise in order to bring the individual in question to book." The impostor Orton is turned over, in a single gesture, to the reading public and to the police. And what follows Greenwood's self-congratulatory acknowledgement of his agency is Orton's signed confession—the signature juridically reproduced at the close of Greenwood's chapter—serving both as an entertainment in the popular interest and as an instrument of indictment.[9]

Greenwood's gesture toward justification is a momentary confession on his own part of the "power of writing" that he exercises; his documentation of London mysteries, in *Low-Life Deeps* and in his earlier *The Wilds of London* (1874), is also a kind of victimization. More often, however, the victimization is less explicit; the function of supplying an entertainment is more obvious than any overt police action. James, we recall, speaks of "mysteries . . . for every spectator," and it is as a spectacle that the underworld is most frequently represented. Furthermore,

---

9. James Greenwood, *Low-Life Deeps: An Account of the Strange Fish to be Found There* (London: Chatto, 1881), 95.

James's formulation—"mysteries . . . for every spectator" rather than "spectators for every mystery"—points to the constitutive power that the spectator exerts. The watcher produces, and not merely reproduces, what he sees and puts the underworld on stage as a theatrical entertainment.

The "staging" of the underworld is evident in Daniel Joseph Kirwan's *Palace and Hovel* (1870). Kirwan is an unselfconscious curiosity seeker and desires simply "to see something interesting." Presenting a series of underworld "scenes," he records, for example, a visit to a thieves' den, and his account is typical in the way it manages to convert a potentially threatening encounter into a moment of theater. His desire to be entertained is immediately gratified: each of the thieves Kirwan interrogates presents himself as an out-of-work entertainer, and each in turn performs for Kirwan's amusement. Crude and prefaced with excuses, the performances are clearly extemporized; the criminals have readily adopted the roles that Kirwan has implicitly assigned and have cooperated to produce the spectacle he wants to see. The underworld, quite literally, appears as a sort of underground theater. And the play is a power play in another sense as well. Kirwan, like most tourists of the nether regions, is accompanied and protected by a police detective, and the detective has supplied the cue for the performance that results. Before admitting the visitors, the "master of the mansion" has asked whether it is "bizness or pleasure," adding that "hif hits business you must 'elp yourself." "O, pleasure by all means," the detective replies.[10] The displacement of poverty and crime into theater, of business into pleasure, is clearly marked, and the performers are willing to confine themselves to the roles of a beggars' opera in order to escape a more definitive confinement.

The metaphor of the theater also pervades Sims's *The Mysteries of Modern London*. His intent is to take the reader "behind the scenes": "When the interior of a house is set upon the stage, the

---

10. Daniel Joseph Kirwan, *Palace and Hovel; or, Phases of London Life*, ed. A. Allan (1870; reprint ed., London: Abelard-Schuman, 1963), 27.

fourth wall is always down in order that the audience may see what is going on. In real life the dramas within the domestic interior are played with the fourth wall up. . . . care is taken that no passer-by shall have a free entertainment. I am going to take the fourth wall down to-day."[11] Indeed, this is not "free entertainment" but the basis of a literary industry; poverty, conspiracy, criminality are purchasable spectacles, at once opened to the public and reduced and distanced as theater. " 'Do show me some cases of unmitigated misery,' is a request said to have been made by a young lady in search of sensation," Mrs. Bernard Bosanquet records in *Rich and Poor* (1896), her study of the slums.[12] The request might easily be that of James's Princess, who "liked seeing queer types and exploring out-of-the-way social corners" (2:234).

But if Sims's fantasy of disclosure—his taking down of the fourth wall—has an immediate theatrical reference, it refers also to another sort of fantasy. The source of Sims's passage might well be the familiar passage in Dickens's *Dombey and Son* in which the author imagines "a good spirit who would take the housetops off . . . and show a Christian people what dark shapes issue from amidst their homes."[13] There is, however, a more immediate source than this fantasy of a providential supervision, a possible source that makes unmistakable the nexus of policing and entertainment I have been tracing: "If we could fly out of that window hand in hand, hover over this great city, gently remove the roofs, and peep in at the queer things which are going on, the strange coincidences, the plannings, the cross-purposes, the wonderful chain of events . . . , it would make all fiction, with its conventionalities and foreseen conclusions, most stale and unprofitable."[14] The speaker is Sherlock Holmes, in A. Conan

---

11. Sims, *The Mysteries of Modern London*, 141.

12. Mrs. Bernard Bosanquet, *Rich and Poor* (London: Macmillan, 1896), 5.

13. Charles Dickens, *Dombey and Son*, New Oxford Illustrated Dickens (London: Oxford University Press, 1950), chap. 47.

14. A. Conan Doyle, *The Sherlock Holmes Illustrated Omnibus* (New York: Schocken, 1976), 31.

Doyle's tale "A Case of Identity," precisely the "police romance" that Sims begins by disavowing and precisely the form that most insistently manifests the twin operations of vision and supervision, of spectatorship and incrimination, that the literature of the underworld engages. The impulse to explore and disclose the underworld in detective fiction becomes indistinguishable from a fantasy of surveillance; in the figure of the detective, seeing becomes the mode of power par excellence.

In "The Adventure of the Copper Beeches," Watson confesses to an uneasiness about sensationalizing the netherworld similar to that found in Sims and Greenwood. Holmes's alibi is exemplary: "You can hardly be open to a charge of sensationalism," he maintains, "for out of these cases . . . , a fair proportion do not treat of crime, in its legal sense, at all." Holmes, as everyone knows, repeatedly acts to mark a separation between his own activities and those of the police detective, and he claims repeatedly that his interest is in those matters "outside the pale of the law."[15] But his investigations appear less to stand "outside" the law than to operate as a more efficient extension of the law. If Holmes's policing is extralegal, it registers an expansion and dissemination of policing techniques and of the apparatus of incrimination: an extension that places even what is avowedly legal within the boundaries of a generalized power of surveillance. Crime, in Holmes's sense, has been redefined to include an expanding range of activities, a shift that moves toward the placing of every aspect of everyday life under suspicion and under investigation.

Such a dream of absolute surveillance and supervision is enacted by the literature that the sensational accounts of London mysteries popularize and supplement: the sociological studies of the underworld that began accumulating in the mid-century with the work of the local statistical societies, Thomas Beames's *The Rookeries of London* (1850) and Henry Mayhew's *London Labour and the London Poor* (1851–1861) and culminating in

---

15. Ibid., 156–57.

Charles Booth's vast *Life and Labour of the People of London* (1889–1903). The sociologist also represents London as a region of mystery to be deciphered, as a largely unexplored and unknown territory; the intent is to "map" the nether world, to place it within the confines of the "known world." As Asa Briggs suggests, "there was a dominating emphasis on 'exploration.' The 'dark city' and the 'dark continent' were alike mysterious, and it is remarkable how often the exploration of the unknown city was compared with the exploration of Africa and Asia."[16] William Booth's *In Darkest England* (1890), for instance, opens with an extended analogy between the exploration for the sources of the Nile in Africa and the exploration for the sources of poverty and criminality in London. Similarly, Jack London, in his study of the London slums, *The People of the Abyss* (1903), equates investigating London and colonial exploration: "But O Cook, O Thomas Cook & Son, pathfinders and trail-clearers . . . , unhesitatingly and instantly, with ease and celerity, could you send me to Darkest Africa or Innermost Thibet, but to the East End of London . . . you know not the way."[17]

As the reference to Cook indicates, exploration of the city appears as a specialized and exotic species of tourism even as it displays a "colonial" attitude toward the underworld. The secretary of a London Workman's Association, H. J. Pettifer, articulated in 1884 one form that this colonial tourism was taking: the urban sociologists, who in the absence of institutional funding required substantial personal wealth to undertake their studies, "had been talking of the working classes as though they were some new-found race, or extinct animal."[18] Reduced to the status of the colonized primitive or "natural curiosity," the "strange fish" of London's "low-life deeps" are collected as exotic "spec-

---

16. Asa Briggs, *Victorian Cities* (London: Odhams Books, 1963), 60.
17. Jack London, *The People of the Abyss* (London: Arco, 1962), 17–18.
18. H. J. Pettifer, *Transactions*, National Association for the Promotion of Social Science (NAPSS), 1884, as cited in Philip Abrams, *The Origins of British Sociology: 1834–1914* (Chicago: University of Chicago Press, 1968), 51.

imens." Muniment, for instance, in *The Princess Casamassima,*
compares Captain Sholto to a "deep-sea fisherman. . . . He
throws his nets and hauls in the little fishes—the pretty little
shining, wriggling fishes. They are all for [the Princess]; she
swallows 'em down." Hyacinth and Muniment are spoken of as if
they were "a sample out of your shop or a little dog you had for
sale." "You see you do regard me as a curious animal," Hyacinth
complains to the Princess. Sholto and the Princess share a "taste
for exploration" and an appetite for queer types; Sholto hunts
the slums as he does the imperial territories, bringing back tro-
phies and specimens for the Princess (1:258–259, 229, 292).

There is a more than metaphoric resemblance between this
colonial attitude toward the slums and the larger movements of
colonization in the period. William Booth, the founder of the
Salvation Army, worked to establish "missions" in darkest England. The larger program he proposed called for the establishment of a series of colonies—"the City Colony, the Farm Colony,
and the Over-Sea Colony"—to deal with the social question. And
the colonizing of the underworld appears also in a somewhat
different, and more comprehensive, form. Booth complains that
the "colonies of heathens and savages in the heart of our capital . . . attract so little attention," but in fact they were drawing
unprecedented attention. The secret world of London has become, as Booth later admits, an "open secret," and even as the
city continues to be spoken of as an impenetrable enigma, the
enigma has been systematically penetrated.[19]

The statistical inscription and mapping of the city in the later
nineteenth century have been well documented and are part of
what might be called a professionalization of the problem of the
city.[20] From the formation of the Statistical Society in 1834 to
Charles Booth's *Life and Labour,* London was meticulously ex-

19. General [William] Booth, *In Darkest England and the Way Out* (London:
International Headquarters of the Salvation Army, 1890), 90–93, 16, 91.

20. See, for instance: Briggs, *Victorian Cities,* 99; G. M. Young, *Victorian England: Portrait of an Age,* 2d ed. (London: Oxford University Press, 1953), 56; Ruth
Glass, "Urban Sociology in Great Britain: A Trend Report," *Current Sociology* 4:4
(1955), 5–19.

plored, documented, and systematized. The intent, as Philip Abrams has observed, was, in part, to put on record "the mode of existence of different families—meals and menus, clothing and furniture, household routines and division of tasks, religious practices and recreation": in short, a scrutiny and recording in detail of the everyday life of the under classes.[21] There is a preoccupation with statistical and enumerative grids, with the laborious accumulation of detail, with the deployment of a comprehensive system of averages and norms. The investigator constructs an interpretive matrix covering virtually every area and activity in the city, from the average traffic on the London streets and the cubic feet of air circulated in the London tenements to a detailed classification of criminals, delinquents, and other deviants from the specified norm.[22] For the sociologist, as for James's Hoffendahl, "moving ever in a dry statistical and scientific air" "humanity, in his scheme, was classified and subdivided with a truly German thoroughness" (2:137, 55).

In the "amateur" investigations of Sims and in the fictive detective work of Holmes, the potential significance of the most trivial detail instigates a thorough scrutiny and surveillance; in the sociological study, we perceive a more discreet and more comprehensive surveillance, leaving no area of the city uncharted. The professionalization of the city proceeds as a tactful and tactical colonization of the territory, enabling an elaborate regularizing and policing of the city. Crucially, the sociological discourse establishes a normative scenario, a system of norms and deviations that effectively "impose[s] a highly specific grid on the common perception of delinquents."[23] A regulative vi-

---

21. Abrams, *The Origins of British Sociology*, 61.

22. See, for instance: Henry Mayhew, *London Labour and the London Poor*, 4 vols. (London: Griffin, Bohn, 1861–62); Abrams, *The Origins of British Sociology*, 13–30; *Journal of the Statistical Society*, published from 1838, and the *Journal of the Royal Statistical Society*, published from 1887; *Annals of the Royal Statistical Society, 1834–1934* (London: Royal Statistical Society, 1934).

23. Michel Foucault, *Surveiller et punir* (Paris: Gallimard, 1975); my citations are to the English translation by Alan Sheridan, *Discipline and Punish: The Birth of the Prison* (New York: Pantheon, 1977), 286.

sion of the city is imposed, "subordinating in its universality all petty irregularities" and holding forth the possibility of that "one glorious principle of universal and undeviating regularity" that the sociologists envisioned.[24] As the British sociologist Frederic J. Mouat observed in 1885, statistics have passed from a merely descriptive stage and have become prescriptive: "statistics have become parliamentary . . . and administrative."[25]

The articulation of the sociological discourse of the city is coextensive with, and opens the way for, the emergence and dispersal of agencies of social training and social control: the multiplication of workhouses and reformatories, of vocational institutions and of institutions for delinquents, the expansion of the metropolitan police and the penal apparatus.[26] The nominal function of these institutions is to train, to educate, to correct, to reform; but clearly, their effect is to impose a general disciplinary and supervisory authority over areas of urban life that have heretofore evaded scrutiny and control. There is an insistent continuity between the theoretical preoccupation with normative scenarios and the institutionalization of that normative vision. And it is not surprising that when the sociologist proposes a model for urban reform, the model is that of the most highly regulated and supervised institution, the prison and reformatory: "In a well-regulated reformatory may be seen the effect of moral and religious discipline, combined with good sanitary conditions, and a proper union of industrial and intellectual education, upon wayward, ignorant and hardened

24. Herbert Spencer, *Social Statics* (London: J. Chapman, 1851), 293; Henry Thomas Buckle, *History of Civilization in England,* 2 vols. (New York: D. Appleton, 1858–61), 2:472. Spencer and Buckle are cited in Alexander Welsh, *The City of Dickens* (Oxford: Clarendon Press, 1971), 49, 50.

25. "The History of the Statistical Society of London," in *Jubilee Volume of the Statistical Society* (London: Stanford, 1885), 52.

26. In addition to the sources already cited, see: T. F. Reddaway, "London in the Nineteenth Century—II: The Origins of the Metropolitan Police," *The Nineteenth Century and After* 147 (1950), 104–18; Wilbur R. Miller, *Cops and Bobbies: Police Authority in New York and London, 1830–1870* (Chicago: University of Chicago Press, 1977); Leon Radzinowicz, *A History of English Criminal Law and Its Administration from 1750* (London: Stevens, 1956), vol. 3.

natures. Such an institution is a type of the great work before us, for there is nothing done in a reformatory which might not, with proper appliances, be effected for society at large."[27] The prison, with its routines and timetables, with its all-encompassing control and supervision, serves as the ideal model for the city. The regulative vision of the city institutionalizes a regulative supervision.

III

The most evident feature of the discourses of the city that I have been tracing is an insistent watchfulness, a "spy mania," which appears at once as a form of entertainment and as a police action. The twin sites of this obsessive surveillance are the theater and the prison. *The Princess Casamassima* invokes this discursive scenario. James recalled his initial sense of the novel as a self-implicating network of watchers: "To find [Hyacinth's] possible adventure interesting I had only to conceive his watching the same public show, the same innumerable appearances, I had watched myself, and of his watching very much as I had watched" (1:vi). This specular relation is reproduced throughout the novel, explicitly in the figures of the police spy and secret agent, whose disguised presence is always suspected, but also in the more ordinary exchanges of sight in the novel. In *The Princess Casamassima*, seeing and being seen always implicitly involve an actual or potential power play. Hyacinth, typically, promises "himself to watch his playmate [Millicent] as he had never done before. She let him know, as may well be supposed, that she had her eye on *him*, and it must be confessed that as regards the exercise of a right of supervision he had felt himself at a disadvantage ever since the night at the theatre" (2:65). Seeing makes for a "right of supervision" and a power of coercion; it is the nexus of seeing

---

27. G. W. Hastings, *Transactions*, NAPSS, 1857.

and power that I now want to examine in *The Princess
Casamassima.*

Hyacinth dates his "disadvantage" from the "night at the theatre," and it does not take much interpretive pressure to see that
a pervasive theatricality runs through the novel. The governing
mode of interaction between characters involves a series of performances: the characters engage in the "entertainment of
watching" (1:307) as they are alternately recruited "for supplying such entertainment" (1:210). Muniment commandeers Hyacinth "for Rosy's entertainment" (1:253) as Hyacinth is brought
to Medley by the Princess because his *"naïveté* would entertain
her" (2:19). The Princess especially is repeatedly referred to in
theatrical terms as an "actress" performing on the *"mise-en-scène*
of life" (1:268), and her imitation of a small bourgeoise provides
Hyacinth with "the most finished entertainment she had yet
offered him" (2:186).

The insistent theatricality of the novel refers less to any "dramatic analogy" than to the reciprocal watchfulness that invests
every relation in the novel. The theater scenes in the novel enact
an indifferent interchange of audience and play as objects of
observation. The theater is the privileged point of vantage for
an "observation of the London world" (1:189), and if, as Hyacinth notes, "one's own situation seem[ed] a play within the play"
(1:208), it is because one is both spectator and spectacle. It is in
the theater that Hyacinth discovers that he is being watched, that
he has been spotted by Sholto and the Princess, herself "over-
shadowed by the curtain of the box, drawn forward with the
intention of shielding her from the observation of the house"
(1:205). Hyacinth, in the balcony and not in the box, is not
shielded from observation, and his vulnerable position indicates
that, despite the exchanges of performance between characters,
there is a certain asymmetry in this "entertainment of watching."

Hyacinth, "lacking all social dimensions was scarcely a percep-
tible person," and he is gratified that Sholto should "recognise
and notice him" in the theater "because even so small a fact as
this was an extension of his social existence" (1:192). The under

classes "exist" only when they have become the object of regard of the upper classes. But there is a counterside to this visibility. For if to be seen is to exist, it is also to be objectified, fixed, and imprisoned in the gaze of the other. It is to be reduced to the status of a "favourable specimen" (1:257), to "studies of the people—the lower orders" (1:305). In the largest sense, to be seen is to be encompassed by a right of supervision.

To escape supervision, characters cultivate a style of secrecy, adopt disguises in order to see without being seen; and, indeed, seeing without being seen becomes the measure of power in the novel. Hyacinth insistently promotes the secret life, at times with a certain absurdity: "I don't understand everything you say, but I understand everything you hide," Millicent tells Hyacinth. "'Then I shall soon become a mystery to you, for I mean from this time forth to cease to seek safety in concealment. You'll know nothing about me then—for it will be all under your nose" (2:332). If seeing is power, secrecy assumes a paramount value, and if beneath every surface a secret truth is suspected, to allow the "truth" to appear is consummately to disguise it.[28]

The relation between a theatrical secrecy and power is most evident in James's representation of the secret society. Invoking Sims's paranoid vision of London conspiracies, the secret society appears as an almost providential power because it is both pervasively present and invisible:

> The forces secretly arrayed against the present social order were pervasive and universal, in the air one breathed, in the ground one trod, in the hand of an acquaintance that one might touch or the eye of a stranger that might rest a moment on one's own. They were above, below, within, without, in every contact and combination of life; and it was no disproof of them to say it was too odd they should lurk in a particular improbable form. To lurk in improbable forms was precisely their strength. [2:275]

The spy mania is universal; the secret society, arrayed in im-

---

28. Mackenzie discusses the "secret society" in *Communities of Honor and Love in Henry James*, 8–18.

probable disguises, exercises a potentially unlimited surveillance, a potentially unlimited supervision.

There is another species of theater in *The Princess Casamassima*
that makes even more explicit the nexus of seeing and power:
the scene of the prison. Hyacinth's meeting with his mother in
Millbank prison appears as another instance of reciprocal watchfulness: "They had too much the air of having been brought
together simply to look at each other" (1:51). Mrs. Bowerbank,
the jailer, scripts the encounter, staging a confrontation "scene"
and managing the action as an entertainment, expressing "a
desire to make the interview more lively" (1:52). She works to
direct an occasion "wanting in brilliancy" and finally moves to
"abbreviate the scene" (1:53, 56). The prison is a theater of
power. Further, the jailer's visit to Pinnie sets the novel in motion; the novel opens under the shadow and gaze of the prison,
"in the eye of the law" (1:7) and under "the steady orb of justice"
(1:8). And most striking about Mrs. Bowerbank is not merely
her representation of "the cold light of the penal system" and
her "official pessimism" (1:14) but the way in which her unre-
lenting observation of Pinnie and Hyacinth is experienced as an
accusation of guilt and as an arrest by the law. This "emissary of
the law" (1:11) imprisons Pinnie in her gaze, and the dressmaker
is "unable to rid herself of the impression that it was somehow
the arm of the law that was stretched out to touch her" (1:13).
When Hyacinth is produced for the jailer's "inspection," he asks:
"Do you want to see me only to look at me?" (1:18). But "only" to
be seen is already to be inscribed within a coercive power relation, to be placed under surveillance and under arrest. Mrs.
Bowerbank's presence transforms the dressmaker's house into a
prison house. The jailer appears as an "overruling providence"
(1:46); her tone "seemed to refer itself to an iron discipline"
(1:14), and Pinnie can only respond "guiltily" (1:8) to her questioning. Pinnie debates taking the "innocent child" to the prison
and "defended herself as earnestly as if her inconsistency had
been of a criminal cast" (1:11, 30). Indicted by Mrs. Bowerbank's
observation, she attempts to shield herself, imagining the "com-

fort to escape from observation" (1:40), and distracts herself from the "case" "as a fugitive takes to by-paths" (1:22).

Pinnie, however, is not merely victimized and incriminated by the turnkey's legal eye. The jailer's visit disseminates an array of inquisitorial looks, recriminations, and betrayals, as the law stretches to include each character. But the characters are not merely victims; they in turn become "carriers" of the law. The more discreet and more insidious power of the law that Mrs. Bowerbank represents is the power to reproduce and extend the apparatus of surveillance and incrimination into situations that seem radically remote from crime, in the legal sense. The distribution of mechanisms of incrimination works not only to victimize those it stretches out to touch but more significantly to make its victims also its disseminators.

The opening scene of the novel is a concise instance of this "spreading" of the law, and a summary of the plot of the opening section is a summary of the displacement and extension of the techniques of penality that Mrs. Bowerbank incarnates. Pinnie, for instance, is not only incriminated by this emissary of the law: she herself becomes Mrs. Bowerbank's emissary. The jailer "would like to see" Hyacinth, and Pinnie undertakes to "look for the little boy," realizing at the same time that to make Hyacinth "visible" is also to bring him to judgment: as she expresses it, "if you could only wait to see the child I'm sure it would help you to judge" (1:3, 15).

To produce Hyacinth is to bring him to the law, and Pinnie both undertakes to produce him and proceeds to exercise a disciplinary authority of her own. As she obeys Mrs. Bowerbank's injunction to supply Hyacinth, she displaces the injunction onto his playmate, Millicent. She simultaneously places Millicent under the discipline of her observation—waiting "to see if her injunction would be obeyed"—and links this injunction with an appropriately reduced attribution of guilt—"you naughty little girl" (1:5). Millie, in turn, replies with a "gaze of deliberation" and with a refusal to "betray" Hyacinth to this extended arm of the law: "Law no, Miss Pynsent, I never see him" (1:6, 5). When

Hyacinth appears, Pinnie repeats her accusation of Millicent: "Millicent 'Enning's a very bad little girl; she'll come to no good" (1:16). Hyacinth protests and tries to exculpate his friend from a betrayal in which he is implicated; his reply further suggests the displacements of guilt and responsibility that obsessively proliferate in this opening scene: "It came over him," he observes, "that he had too hastily shifted to her shoulders the responsibility of his unseemly appearance, and he wished to make up to her for this betrayal" (1:17).

These shifts and displacements of criminality and incrimination indicate a generalized extension of the power of watching and policing in the novel. In *The Princess Casamassima*, police work is contagious, a contagion that James images as the transmission of a certain "dinginess" from one character to another: Hyacinth "hated people with too few fair interspaces, too many smutches and streaks. Millicent Henning generally had two or three of these at least, which she borrowed from her doll, into whom she was always rubbing her nose and whose dinginess was contagious. It was quite inevitable she should have left her mark under his own nose when she claimed her reward for coming to tell him about the lady who wanted him" (1:17). If Hyacinth has shifted onto Millicent the blame for his "unseemly appearance," leading to Pinnie's accusations of her, the shifting of blame and guilt corresponds to the shifting of a mark of "dinginess," the stigma of the slums.

The opening scene plays out, in an anticipatory and understated fashion, the diffusion of penality that traverses *The Princess Casamassima*. It is the prison that provides the model for the contagion. The first principle of the prison is isolation, confinement, but within the novel Millbank prison stands as the central and centering instance of this spread of criminality; the prison

> looked very sinister and wicked, to Miss Pynsent's eyes, and she wondered why a prison should have such an evil air if it was erected in the interest of justice and order—a builded protest, precisely, against vice and villainy. This particular penitentiary struck her as about as bad and wrong as those who were in it; it

threw a blight on the face of day, making the river seem foul and poisonous and the opposite bank, with a protrusion of long-necked chimneys, unsightly gasometers and deposits of rubbish, wear the aspect of a region at whose expense the jail had been populated. [1:42]

Vice and villainy are not confined by the *cordon sanitaire* of the prison; rather, the prison infects the surrounding area, disperses its "evil air," and blights the city. The prison spreads what it ostensibly protests against and is erected to delimit. The atmosphere of the prison extends from the local site of the prison into every area of the novel, and there is no escape from the contagion of criminality; as Pinnie notes, every "effort of mitigation . . . only involved her more deeply" (1:8).[29] "He had not done himself justice"; "she seemed to plead guilty to having been absurd"; "Hyacinth's terrible cross-questioning"; "he went bail for my sincerity": one might multiply these quotations indefinitely, and I abstract them from their local contexts because it is the multiplication of these references, in the most banal and "innocent" exchanges in the novel, that establishes a general context of policing and incrimination in *The Princess Casamassima*. The very ordinariness of the allusions indicates the extent to which a fantasy of supervision and police work infiltrates the novel.

"What do you mean, to watch me?" Hyacinth asks Mr. Vetch, and the question alludes to more than the fiddler's paternal overseeing of Hyacinth. The possibility that Mr. Vetch is a police spy has earlier been considered; the manner in which the possibility is dismissed extends rather than limits the spy mania that the novel reproduces: Hyacinth

> never suspected Mr. Vetch of being a governmental agent, though Eustache Poupin had told him that there were a great

---

29. On the "Dickensian" theme of a contagious criminality, see, for instance: Michael Ignatieff, *A Just Measure of Pain: The Penitentiary in the Industrial Revolution, 1750–1850* (New York: Pantheon, 1978), 61.

many who looked a good deal like that: not of course with any
purpose of incriminating the fiddler. . . . The governmental
agent in extraordinary disguises . . . became a very familiar type
to Hyacinth, and though he had never caught one of the infamous brotherhood in the act there were plenty of persons to
whom, on the very face of the matter, he had no hesitation in
attributing the character. [1:108]

The secret agent lurks in improbable forms, and as in Sims's
fantasies of the anarchic underworld, apparent innocence invites a suspicion of concealed criminality. This passage denies
suspicion and the purpose of incrimination even as it attributes
the character of the police spy indiscriminately. The attribution
attaches, at one time or another, to virtually every character in
the novel. To Captain Sholto, for instance: "Perhaps you think
he's a spy, an *agent provocateur* or something of the sort." But
Sholto's form is not improbable enough, a spy "would disguise
himself more" (1:214). It attaches also to the Princess, who is
suspected of being "an agent on the wrong side."

The Princess, Madame Grandoni tells the Prince, is "much
entangled. She has relations with people who are watched by the
police." "And is *she* watched by the police?" "I can't tell you; it's
very possible—except that the police here isn't like that of other
countries" (2:310). Indeed, the police here are not like they are
elsewhere—they are everywhere. Just prior to this discussion,
the Princess and Paul Muniment have left the house at Madeira
Crescent on a conspiratorial mission that remains a narrative
secret. The spies are themselves spied upon, as the narrative
observer comments: "Meanwhile, it should be recorded, they
had been followed, at an interval, by a cautious figure, a person
who, in Madeira Crescent, when they came out of the house, was
stationed on the other side of the street, at a considerable distance. On their appearing he had retreated a little, still however
keeping them in sight" (2:301). James initially withholds the
identity of the observer who has placed the conspirators under
surveillance. His revelation of that identity takes a curious form:
"The reader scarce need be informed, nevertheless, that his

design was but to satisfy himself as to the kind of person his wife was walking with" (2:301). The disavowal of any need to inform the reader of the figure's identity only points to the reader's initial misidentification. The passage invites a "confusion" of domestic suspicions and police surveillance and indicates the extent to which all actions in the novel have come to resemble a police action. All characters in the novel are "in danger of playing the spy" (2:348).

There is no space free from the spy mania, from the infection of penality. Medley, the Princess's country-house retreat, provides no escape. The Princess there informs Hyacinth that "I've been watching you. I'm frank enough to tell you that. I want to see more—more—more!" (2:36). And if Hyacinth ceases "to be insignificant from the moment" the Princess sees him, he experiences his accession to significance as a subjection to "cross-examination" (2:35). A dispersed surveillance shadows Hyacinth, both in the Princess's watchfulness and in the supervision of his conduct "under the eye of the butler" (2:41). Medley is, for Hyacinth, the "real country," real nature, but nature itself participates in the general police action: "Never had the old oaks and beeches . . . witnessed such an extraordinary series of confidences since the first pair that sought isolation wandered over the grassy slopes and ferny dells beneath them" (2:46).

The witnessing eye of nature and the allusion to the providential supervision of the Garden indicate the thorough "naturalization" of mechanisms of surveillance and policing in *The Princess Casamassima*: nature itself appears to supplement the policing function. Mrs. Bowerbank early comments on Florentine's impending death by asserting that "if she lived a month [she] would violate (as Mrs. Bowerbank might express herself) every established law of nature" (1:14). James's parenthetical interpolation calls attention to the jailer's characteristic mode of expression, her linking of "nature" and the "law," her naturalizing of the penal apparatus. In *The Princess Casamassima*, the power of vision and supervision is not confined to the nominal agencies of the police: it is enforced by the "eyes of the world" (2:401). It is finally impossible to distinguish between the "eye of day and the observation of the police" (2:410).

IV

The spy mania and the incriminating techniques of policing and surveillance are not confined but contagious in *The Princess Casamassima;* the prison and the supervision and discipline it implies reappear at every turn in the novel. I have indicated the proposal of the prison as a model for the city at large in the work of the London sociologists, and I now want to take up the significance of this equation from a somewhat different perspective. Michel Foucault, in *Surveiller et punir,* his recent history of the rise of disciplinary practices, describes the extension of social mechanisms of surveillance and discipline into all areas of modern society. More specifically, he traces the reorganization of Western society around the model of the "punitive city": "Near at hand, sometimes even at the very centre of cities of the nineteenth century [stands] the monotonous figure, at once material and symbolic, of the power to punish"—the prison. The architectural figure of this social reorganization is Jeremy Bentham's Panopticon, a circular building, divided into cells, surrounding a central observation tower. The Panopticon operates through a controlling network of seeing and being seen: the inmate "is seen, but he does not see"; "in the central tower, one sees everything without ever being seen." The inmate is trapped in a "seeing machine," trapped in a state of conscious and constant visibility; as a result, he "inscribes in himself the power relation" in which he is caught up and "becomes the principle of his own subjection."[30]

London's Millbank prison was derived from Bentham's pan-

---

30. Foucault, *Discipline and Punish,* 116, 200, 202, 207, 202–203. On the Panopticon, see also: Gertrude Himmelfarb, "The Haunted House of Jeremy Bentham," in her *Victorian Minds* (New York: Alfred A. Knopf, 1968).

opticon scheme. Convicts were accommodated in six pentagonal ranges that surrounded a central watchtower—the locus of a providential supervision that doubled also, and appropriately, as the prison chapel. James visited Millbank on a December morning in 1884 to collect notes for *The Princess Casamassima*. His description of the prison in the novel emphasizes the power of watching that the Panopticon employs. He records the "circular shafts of cells" ranged about a central observatory and, further, the "opportunity of looking at captives through grated peepholes," at the women with "fixed eyes" that Pinnie is "afraid to glance at" (1:47); the inmates are dressed in "perfect frights of hoods" (1:46). This last detail recalls the practice at Pentonville, where "all contact with other human beings, except the prison staff, was forbidden, and when convicts left their cells . . . , they wore masks with narrow eye-slits in order to prevent identification by their fellows."[31]

The Panopticon effects an exemplary conjunction of seeing and power, the conjunction that extends from the prison throughout *The Princess Casamassima*. "The panoptic schema," Foucault details, ". . . was destined to spread throughout the social body." Foucault discusses the dispersal of this schema in nineteenth-century society, its penetration into the factory, the workhouse, the reformatory, the school—into, in fact, all those institutions that, as we have seen, the urban colonizers deployed and cultivated. And further, the panoptic technique infiltrates "tiny, everyday" social practices, traverses and embraces those "minute social disciplines" apparently remote from the scene of the prison. Confiscating and absorbing "things of every moment," an everyday panopticism is finally universalized: "Police power must bear 'over everything.' "[32]

One final institutionalization of the panoptic technology remains to be considered. It has recently been suggested that Foucault's history might underwrite a radical revision of our

31. Sheppard, *London, 1808–1870: The Infernal Wen*, 375–77.
32. Foucault, *Discipline and Punish*, 207, 213, et passim. See also Jacques Donzelot, *La police des familles* (Paris: Editions de Minuit, 1977).

sense of the "politics" of the novel, and the problem that I want now to take up, and which has been implicit all along, concerns the relation between these disciplinary techniques and the techniques of the novel, and more particularly of the realist and naturalist novel, which appears on the scene at the same time that the disciplinary society takes power.[33] Foucault suggests that the novel "forms part of that great system of constraint by which the West compelled the everyday to bring itself into discourse."[34] In what way may the realist novel be seen to participate in, and even to promote, a system of constraint?

It has been observed that "excellence of *vision* is the distinguishing mark of realism."[35] "To see" is the dominant verb in the realist text—"la gastronomie de l'oeil," as Balzac expressed it[36]—and realist fiction is preeminently concerned with seeing, with a seeing in detail. The proximity of this realist "seeing" to the overseeing and police work of detection becomes explicitly problematic and is most evident, of course, in the subgenre of realism that we have already glanced at, the fiction of detection.[37] In detective fiction, the relation between seeing and policing is taken for granted; literally, the range of the detective's

33. I am indebted especially to Leo Bersani, "The Subject of Power," *Diacritics* 7:3 (1977), 2–21; D. A. Miller, "From *roman-policier* to *roman-police:* Wilkie Collins's *The Moonstone*," *Novel* 13 (1980), 153–170; and Miller's "The Novel and the Police," *Glyph 8: Johns Hopkins Textual Studies* (Baltimore: Johns Hopkins University Press, 1981). See also: Jonathan Arac, *Commissioned Spirits: The Shaping of Social Motion in Dickens, Carlyle, Melville, and Hawthorne* (New Brunswick: Rutgers University Press, 1979), esp. chap. 1; Paul Foss, "The Lottery of Life," in *Michel Foucault: Power, Truth, Strategy*, ed. Meaghan Morris and Paul Patton (Sydney: Feral, 1979); Jeffrey Mehlman, *Revolution and Repetition: Marx/Hugo/Balzac* (Berkeley: University of California Press, 1977), 123–24; and Lennard J. Davis, "Wicked Actions and Feigned Words: Criminals, Criminality, and the Early English Novel," *Yale French Studies* 59 (1980), 106–18.

34. Foucault, "The Life of Infamous Men," in *Michel Foucault: Power, Truth, Strategy*, 91.

35. Mehlmann, *Revolution and Repetition*, 124.

36. Balzac, cited in Donald Fanger, *Dostoevsky and Romantic Realism* (Cambridge: Harvard University Press, 1965), 30.

37. On the detective story, see Miller, "From *roman-policier* to *roman-police:* Wilkie Collins's *The Moonstone*"; and Pierre Macherey, *A Theory of Literary Production*, trans. Geoffrey Wall (London: Routledge, 1978), 18–36.

vision is the range of his power. That power operates by placing the entire world of the text under scrutiny and under surveillance and invokes the possibility of an absolute supervision, in which everything may be comprehended and "policed" and in which the most trifling detail becomes potentially incriminating. Realistic fiction, in a more discreet and, for that reason, more comprehensive manner, deploys a similar tactic of detection; the techniques of surveillance and detection traverse the techniques of the realistic novel. Emerson, instancing Swift, notes "how realistic or materialistic in treatment of his subject" the novelist is: "He describes his fictitious persons as if for the police."[38] Indeed, detective fiction merely literalizes the realist representational scrutiny, its fascination with seeing and with the telling significance of detail, and lays bare *the policing of the real* that is the realist project. "We novelists," writes Zola, "are the examining magistrates of men and their passions."[39]

The juridical expression of the aims of the realist novelist recurs frequently. There is, for instance, George Eliot's statement in *Adam Bede* (chapter 17) of the novelist's obligation to write "as if I were in the witness-box narrating my experience on oath" and Guy de Maupassant's avowal, in his preface to *Pierre et Jean*, to tell "la vérité, rien que la vérité, et toute la vérité."[40] And earlier, there is Lamb's comment that reading Defoe "is like reading evidence in a court of Justice" or Hazlitt's observation that Richardson "sets about describing every object and transaction, as if the whole had been given in on evidence by an eyewitness."[41] The convergence of the literary and the legal recurs also in attacks on the alleged illicitness and "illegality" of the

---

38. Ralph Waldo Emerson, *English Traits*, in *The Selected Writings of Ralph Waldo Emerson*, ed. Brooks Atkinson (New York: Modern Library, 1950), 647.

39. Emile Zola, "The Experimental Novel," in *Documents of Modern Literary Realism*, ed. George J. Becker (Princeton: Princeton University Press, 1963), 168.

40. George Eliot, *Adam Bede*, ed. Stephen Gill (Harmondsworth: Penguin, 1980), chap. 17; Guy de Maupassant, *Pierre et Jean* New York: Scribner's, 1936), xxxvi.

41. Charles Lamb and William Hazlitt cited in Ian Watt, *The Rise of the Novel* (Berkeley: University of California Press, 1957), 34.

realistic novel; thus W. S. Lilly, writing in 1885, asserts that, in the realist and naturalist novel, "everywhere at the bottom there is filth (*l'ordure*). Those proceedings in the courts of justice which from time to time bring it to the surface—like an abscess—are merely an experimental novel unfolding itself, chapter after chapter, before the public."[42] The realist novel is seen to proceed as a legal action. The realist novelist is the examining magistrate of everyday life.

There is a complementary movement in realistic fiction: toward a documentation of phenomena in precise detail, and toward a supervision of these phenomena. As Zola concisely expresses it, "the goal of the experimental method . . . is to study phenomena in order to control them."[43] The realists share, with other colonizers of the urban scene, a passion to see and document "things as they are," and this passion takes the form of a fantasy of surveillance, a placing of the tiniest details of everyday life under scrutiny. Is it not possible to discover in this fantasy of surveillance a point of intersection between the realist text and a society increasingly dominated by institutions of discipline, regularization, and supervision—by the dispersed networks of the "police"?

There are a number of ways in which the relation between the novel and the law can be explored. There is, for instance, an intriguing resemblance between the realist typologies of character and the typologies proposed by the late nineteenth-century criminologists, chiefly Cesare Lombroso, a resemblance that Conrad exploits in *The Secret Agent*, another novel of the London

---

42. W. S. Lilly, "The New Naturalism," in *Documents of Modern Literary Realism*, ed. Becker, 277. Perhaps the most extraordinary indictment of the realist and naturalist novelists occurs in Max Nordau's influential *Degeneration* (New York: D. Appleton, 1895). Nordau classifies these novelists, preeminently Zola, in accordance with the classification of criminal types developed by the criminologist Cesare Lombroso, accuses them of "crime committed with pen and crayon" (p. 558), and calls for the institution of a "critical police" (p. 535) to return them to the law; at the same time, however, Nordau notes the resemblance between the realist text and the "police reports" (p. 489).

43. Zola, "The Experimental Novel," 176.

spy mania.[44] More generally, one might note the encompassing control over character and action that the realist and naturalist doctrine of "determinism" secures. As Leo Bersani has recently suggested, the realist's method works to reduce "the events of fiction to a parade of sameness. For example, it would not be wholly absurd to suggest that a Balzac novel becomes unnecessary as soon as its exposition is over. The entire work is already contained in the presentation of the work, and the characters merely repeat in dialogue and action what has already been established about them in narrative summaries. Their lives mirror the expository portraits made of them at the beginning of the novel."[45]

The linear order and progression of the realistic novel enable the novel to "progress" only in a direction always preestablished. Indeed, it is as a "repetition" that Hyacinth experiences his every attempt to break with his origins and "antecedents," to break with his "naturalist" determinants of environment and heredity. His recruitment to assassinate the duke presents itself as "the idea of a *repetition*," as the "horror of the public reappearance, in his person, of the imbrued hands of his mother" (2:419). This "young man in a book" (1:xiv) expresses an interest in the "advanced and consistent realists" (1:315), but this "consistency," a key word in the novel, becomes another name for an entrapment in a (narrative) repetition.

In its fixing of consistent "types," and in its predictive control over narrative possibility, the realistic text gains a thorough mastery over its characters and their actions—a twin mastery of intelligibility and supervision. *The Princess Casamassima* has been regarded as James's primary excursion into the realistic or naturalistic mode.[46] The novel, in its choice of subjects and in its

44. On Conrad's use of Lombroso, see John E. Saveson, "Conrad, *Blackwood's*, and Lombroso," *Conradiana* 6 (1974), 57–62.

45. Leo Bersani, *Baudelaire and Freud* (Berkeley: University of California Press, 1977), 121.

46. Lyall H. Powers, in *Henry James and the Naturalist Movement*, claims that

descriptive method, displays an affinity with the consistent realists, and certainly, it everywhere displays the fantasy of surveillance which, I have been suggesting, lies at the heart of the realist project. But we notice that this surveillance becomes in many ways the subject and not merely the mode of the novel, and such a foregrounding of the novel's tactics of supervision indicates, within limits that I will attempt to describe, James's exposure and demystification of the realist mania for surveillance and his attempt to disown the policing that it implies.

Perhaps the most powerful tactic of supervision achieved by the traditional realist novel inheres in its dominant technique of narration—the style of "omniscient narration" that grants the narrative voice an unlimited authority over the novel's "world," a world thoroughly known and thoroughly mastered by the panoptic "eye" of the narration. The technique of omniscient narration, as is frequently noted, gives to the narrator a providential vision of the characters and action. It is the fantasy of such an absolute panopticism that we have previously traced in Sims's lifting of the fourth wall, and in Dickens's and Doyle's fantasy of "removing the roofs" and viewing the "queer things which are going on." In *The Princess Casamassima,* such omniscient vision is attributed to the master revolutionaries: "They know everything—everything. They're like the great God of the believers: they're searchers of hearts; and not only of hearts, but of all a man's life—his days, his nights, his spoken, his unspoken words. Oh they go deep and they go straight!" (2:383). Hoffendahl's God-like power is also the power of the omniscient narrator, a power of unlimited overseeing.

But if James inscribes in his text an image of comprehensive and providential supervision, the narrative method of the novel departs from this panoptic technique. As a number of critics

---

James had, by the mid-1880s, "made his peace" with the naturalists: "He had by this time come close to sharing fully the aesthetic persuasions of the Realist-Naturalist group" (p. 41). It is, rather, James's attempts to disaffiliate himself from the realist and naturalist "group," and from the politics that their method implies, that I emphasize here.

have shown, and as James asserts in his preface to the novel, *The Princess Casamassima* marks a technical turning point in James's career: a turning away from the style of omniscient narration toward the technique of the "central recording consciousness" or "central intelligence." That technique displaces the authority of the narrative voice and disavows any direct interpretive authority over the action. It can be said that in *The Princess Casamassima*, omniscient authority is held up to scrutiny, and indicted, in being transferred to, or displaced upon, the masters of the revolution.

Can this supervisory power, however, be so easily disowned? In his preface, James imagines his observation of the underworld as a form of espionage: his vision of London is that of "the habitual observer . . . the pedestrian prowler" (1:xxi-xxii). But at the same time, he disclaims any violation or manipulation of the figures he "merely" observes: "I recall pulling no wires, knocking at no closed doors, applying for no 'authentic' information" (1:xxii). It is Hoffendahl, in the novel, who is the arch wire puller: "He had in his hand innumerable other threads" (2:55). And it is this puppeteering that James disavows. But having denied such a manipulative power, James proceeds to reclaim what he has dismissed: "To haunt the great city and by this habit to penetrate it, imaginatively, in as many places as possible—*that* was to be informed, *that* was to pull wires, *that* was to open doors" (1:xxii).

James distinguishes his "imaginative" penetration of the city from the manipulative vision and supervision of the conspiratorial plotters. The implication is clear: James would claim that his imaginative wire pulling is not an act of supervision, that his deep searching of hearts, of spoken and unspoken words, that his seeing and "haunting" of the city can be distinguished from the policing and spy mania that this haunting of the great city so closely resembles. It is just such a separation between "mere" seeing, consciousness, and knowledge and an exercise of power that I have been questioning. James offers the alibi of a "powerless" imagination to extricate himself from the charge of

participating in the spy mania that the novel everywhere engages. But James would have no need to insist on the distinction
if it were not already jeopardized, already threatened by the
compelling resemblance between his haunting and perpetual
prowling and the surveillance and policing from which he would
disengage himself.

It becomes clear that the attempt on the part of the writers we
have examined to disown the policing that they exercise can be
seen as a "cover" for a more discreet and comprehensive policy
of supervision, and it is as such a ruse that I think James's displacing of power and authority works. The recession of narrative supervision in *The Princess Casamassima* appears as one
further "shifting of the shame," a displacing of responsibility,
culpability, and, in the terms which the novel provides, criminality. The shifting of narrative authority makes reference to an
uneasiness concerning the shame of power. If James's novel is
systematically the story of a criminal continuity between seeing
and power, this continuity is finally disowned. If James works
toward a demystifying of the realist policing of the real, this
police work is finally remystified, recuperated as the "innocent"
work of the imagination.

From one point of view, the incompatibility of the novel and
the subject of power is the "message" of *The Princess Casamassima:* the incompatibility of aesthetic and political claims
leads to Hyacinth's suicide. Critics of the novel have restated this
message, insisting, with approval or disapprobation, that the
novel sacrifices its political references to technical preoccupations. In his preface, James himself observes that the underworld of London "lay heavy on one's consciousness" (1:vi). The
phrase invites us to read "conscience" for "consciousness," and
the substitution registers in miniature what has been seen as
James's substitution in *The Princess Casamassima* of the ordeal of
consciousness (that is, the work's technique) for matters of social
conscience (its political subject). Thus it has been argued that
"Hyacinth Robinson's sensitive consciousness is the mirror
which controls the shape" of the novel, that James's "ignorance

in the face of the reality, the great grey Babylon, which was nearest to him," compelled him to distort that reality by circumscribing it with a "controlling and bizarre consciousness," and that, finally, this technical preoccupation means that *The Princess Casamassima's* "theme is not political at all."[47] As Leo Bersani points out, "it has been decided by 'politically conscious' Anglo-American critics that James is a nonpolitical novelist."[48]

Critics of *The Princess Casamassima,* and of James's work generally, have restated the discontinuity that James himself proposed, enforcing a break between technique and subject, between ways of seeing and the subject of power. It is maintained that "in his quest for a quintessential social reality that was also an alien reality, James must necessarily have found himself recoiling upon the merely psychological and even epistemological, the merely imaginative—upon fantasy."[49] But if James's only "political novel" advertises a radical conflict between politics and the novel, there is, working against this simple polarization, a criminal continuity between the techniques of the novel and the social technologies of power that inhere in these techniques. It is in this rigorous continuity established in James's novels between seeing, knowing, and exercising power that the politics of the Jamesian text appears, and it is this continuity that I have been tracing in *The Princess Casamassima.*

James closes his preface to *The Princess Casamassima* by acknowledging an apparently disqualifying lack of knowledge about his ostensible subject. The setting of the novel is the anarchic underworld of London, but the scene of writing is far removed from the scene of the action: "I remember at any rate feeling myself all in possession of little Hyacinth's consistency, as I have called it, down at Dover during certain weeks that were

---

47. The quotations are from, respectively: J. M. Leucke, "*The Princess Casamassima:* Hyacinth's Fallible Consciousness," in *Henry James: Modern Judgments,* ed. Tony Tanner (London: Macmillan, 1969), 184; John Goode, "The Art of Fiction: Walter Besant and Henry James," 280, 279; J. A. Ward, *The Search for Form* (Chapel Hill: University of North Carolina Press, 1967), 115.

48. Bersani, "The Subject of Power," 10.

49. Mackenzie, *Communities of Honor and Love in Henry James,* 22.

none too remotely precedent to the autumn of 1885 and the appearance, in 'The Atlantic Monthly' again, of the first chapters of the story" (1:xx). Like the Princess, James appears to have "retired to a private paradise to think out the problem of the slums." But even here James obliquely acknowledges a continuity between this scene of light and culture and the policed underworld of London. The law reappears even in the midst of this private paradise: "There were certain sunny, breezy balconied rooms at the quieter end of the Esplanade of that cheerful castle-crested little town—now infinitely perturbed by gigantic 'harbour works,' but then only faded and over-soldiered and all pleasantly and humbly submissive to the law that snubs in due course the presumption of flourishing resorts" (1:xx). "Oversoldiered" and "humbly submissive to the law," in the diffused and extended sense that the novel has promoted, the scene of writing is a muted repetition of the scene of the novel. Reinscribed in the ordinary and everyday, the "police" are everywhere.

2

"The Vigilance of 'Care'": Love and Power in *The Golden Bowl*

I

"English liberty is a method, not a goal," George Santayana observes in his essay "English Liberty in America": "It is related to the value of human life very much as the police are related to public morals or commerce to wealth; and it is no accident that the Anglo-Saxon race excels in commerce . . . and that having policed itself successfully it is beginning to police the world." If such a relation between liberty and domestic and imperial policing seems somewhat startling, it derives from what Santayana sees as the peculiar character of "freedom" in England and America. This species of liberty, he argues, involves not an "heroic" and uncompromising "love of freedom"—what Santayana calls "primitive liberty"—but rather "co-operation" and "compromise." Anglo-Saxon liberty is essentially a mechanism of "accommodation." It operates by promoting a comprehensive "moral unison" and subsists "by a mechanical equilibrium of habits and interests." The social equilibrium thus effected appears as a state of "general harmony," and potentially dispersive interests are brought into balance by a spirit of partnership and mutual concern through which "good manners and generous feelings are diffused among the people." Even Anglo-Saxon imperialism is mannerly and generous. A scheme of benevolent cooperation and "happy unison," it is "essentially an invitation to pull together." And this scheme of domination, this method of liberty, is eminently successful: "To dominate the world, cooperation is better than policy."[1]

If Anglo-Saxon liberty is not a goal but a method, this is because the method is already the goal. Santayana equates liberty with commerce and policing because all work as mechanisms of regulation, securing interests, morality, and wealth, not through *external* interventions or coercions but through *internal* tactics of adjustment and correction. The mechanical equilibrium of the Anglo-Saxon scheme, like the clockwork mechanism to which it was often compared, appears all but self-regulating.[2] Thus, for Santayana, the Anglo-Saxon method of liberty is so effective that it renders "overt government unnecessary." More precisely, a covert mode of governing is already in place, a discreet set of controls that guarantees that the invitation to "pull together" is accepted. The organic unity of the Anglo-Saxon style of domination is in fact achieved through a regime of "overwhelming compulsions." Prohibitions are scarce in England and especially in America, but they are rendered almost superfluous by a general network of "compulsions"; and, as Santayana notes, "prohibitions are less galling than compulsions": "What can be forbidden specifically . . . may be avoided by a prudent man without renouncing the whole movement of life and mind. . . . what is exacted cuts deeper; it creates habits which overlay nature, and every faculty is atrophied that does not conform with them."[3]

The weakness of prohibitions lies not merely in their specifici-

1. George Santayana, *Character and Opinion in the United States* (New York: Scribner's, 1920), 199–208.

2. For an account of commerce and economics as mechanisms of regulation and equilibration, see Albert O. Hirschman, *The Passions and the Interests: Political Arguments for Capitalism before Its Triumph* (Princeton: Princeton University Press, 1977), 48–63, 69–87.

3. Santayana, *Character and Opinion*, 207, 209–10.

ty—what can be localized can be avoided—but also in their ad-
ventitious application. Prohibitions simply say "no"; they are
extra-ordinary and imposed "from the outside." On the contrary, compulsions, neither local nor merely negative, invest and
constitute the ordinary and the normal, regulating the "whole
movement of life and mind." What is *ir*regular, what does not
conform, what violates the formal equilibrium, simply "atro-
phies." Anglo-Saxon power is, in the sense I have already begun
to suggest in the preceding chapter, a power of *normalization,* a
disciplinary method that induces conformity and regulation not
by levying violence but through an immanent array of norms
and compulsions. The "health" of the social body is ensured
through a homeostatic technique of adjustment and organic
conformation. Policing is thoroughly internalized, and if in England and in America one need "never hear of the police," it is
because everyone is free to police himself.[4]

Such a balanced economy of freedom and supervision—an
immanent policing so thoroughly inscribed in the most ordinary
social practices that it is finally indistinguishable from manners,
cooperation, and care—constitutes, I want to suggest, both the
subject and mode of *The Golden Bowl.* For James as for Santayana, the secret of the "national genius" and of the "national
success" of the English is "their wonderful spirit of compromise," their instinct for the equilibrium. This mechanism of equilibrium centers the novel: on one level, it is Maggie Verver who
perfects a method of supervised freedom, at once producing in
her subjects "the sense of highly choosing" and exercising control by invoking the regulative power of the norm; on another, it
is the Jamesian imperative of organic form that underwrites and
ratifies this system of supervision.[5]

But these complementary strategies of control hardly appear
as such. One of the most extraordinary passages in *The Golden*

---

4. Ibid., 207.
5. Henry James, *The Golden Bowl* (New York: Scribner's, 1909), 1:354. Subsequent references to the novel and to the preface are to this edition (vols. 23 and
24 of the New York Edition) and appear in parentheses in the text.

Bowl appears just after Fanny Assingham has shattered the gilded bowl and Maggie has informed the Prince that she "knows." Fanny reflects on Maggie's precarious maintenance of the "precious equilibrium" of the marriages, an equilibrium kept up through the Princess's "paramount law" of discretion. Conforming to this law and observing Maggie's tactical rule of tact, Fanny "knew accordingly nothing but harmony, she diffused restlessly nothing but peace—an extravagant expressive aggressive peace, not incongruous after all with the solid calm of the place; a kind of helmeted, trident-shaking *pax Britannica*" (2:209). Not merely does this passage equate Maggie's domestic policy of "diplomacy" (2:210) with the power strategies of the Imperium; it further suggests that the single term that subsumes both the Princess's aggressive micropolitics and the general politics of Empire is peace, "nothing but peace."

The Golden Bowl is a novel about power—conjugal, commercial, and imperial—but throughout the novel power is represented in terms of "mildness," "harmony," and "calm." More precisely, the name that James gives to the exercising of power in *The Golden Bowl* is love. Maggie acts all "for love" (2:116). "Silent and discreet," she consistently displays a "vague mild face" and diffuses a benevolent decorum. But clearly her mildness and benevolence operate also as a strategy of control. Acting always "in the name of the equilibrium" (2:18), Maggie works to reform and to correct the perverse form that the marriages have taken, to restore the "group normally constituted" (2:146). Yet if her actions signify to the adulterers Amerigo and Charlotte that "she wished them well" (2:234), it is through this care that she imposes her will. She simply loves, and "that's how I make them do what I like!" (2:115). I want to examine this entanglement between love and power in *The Golden Bowl*.

The well-policed character of the "world" of *The Golden Bowl* is at once readily apparent and difficult to assess, apparent in that the novel everywhere displays the nexus of seeing, knowing, and exercising power that, I have argued, defines the politics of the Jamesian text, problematic in that police work and supervision in the novel are so thoroughly inscribed in gestures of compassion, care, and love. It is not hard to see that the space the characters in the novel inhabit is a "watching space" (1:98) and that the characters engage in struggles to see and to know that establish relations of constant surveillance and "mutual vigilance" (2:267). This vigilance opens up the possibility that the most trifling detail might "become a sign" (1:154), betray a significance in the general semiotics of detection and exposure that inscribes the world of the novel. Seeing, in *The Golden Bowl* as in *The Princess Casamassima*, constitutes the central narrative action, and the process of vision everywhere entails a power of supervision.

But policing in *The Golden Bowl* operates in a markedly different register than in the earlier novel. The explicit and "official" agencies of the law retain a more than nominal presence in *The Princess Casamassima*. The text registers a dispersal of policing functions into the most everyday exchanges in the novel, but the subject of power is still overtly caught up with the topics of the law, the prison, and the police. Power in James's novel of the London underworld is always referred back to the penal technologies that traverse the text; James at once invokes and disavows this negative, legal, and prohibitory version of power. The "positive" techniques of regulation in the late fiction, on the contrary, make for a virtual disappearance of the traditional institutions of power, an elision of the avowed offices of the law (the detective and the divorce court, for instance) and, collaterally, of the omniscient and panoptic narration that supplements them.

The elision is possible not because policing has been restricted or excluded from the world of the novel—"People are always traceable, in England," as Fanny points out, "when tracings are required" (2:134)—but because supervisory functions have been comprehensively taken over by other less obtrusive, less "shameful" networks of surveillance. Certainly, vestiges of the "older" economy of power survive in *The Golden Bowl*, most evidently in the roles played by the Assinghams as narrative overseers, providentially "watching over them *all*" (2:124). It is appropriately Colonel Assingham, the retired policeman of the Empire, who, at the great party at which the Prince and Charlotte first appear conspicuously together, keeps his "lonely vigil" from his position "aloft in his gallery" (1:249). The Colonel resembles a person "in charge of the police arrangements or the electric light," in charge both of making visible and of "looking down" on the exposed Charlotte in a manner that notifies her that she will be "suspected, sounded, veritably arraigned" (1:249). Fanny's "attentive arrest" (1:251) and cross-examination of Charlotte quickly reveal an inadequacy, however, and the defect lies not in the impossibility of disclosing the adulterous pair but precisely in the danger of such a disclosure.

"The overt recognition of danger was worse than anything else" (1:273), both for the "mistake" in which it would implicate Fanny and, more significantly, for the threat it would pose to the ostensible peace and equilibrium of the marriages. Fanny's too-evident policing intentions violate just that "value of Discretion" that everywhere characterizes the novel's regulative policies.[6] It is the very overtness of this overseeing and arraigning that the narrative disowns. One might even say that Fanny experiences a certain nostalgia for the old regime of the law. When she returns from the party, and "when the carriage happened . . . to catch the straight shaft from the lamp of a policeman in the act of playing his inquisitive flash over an opposite house-front, she let herself wince at being thus incriminated only that she might protest, not less quickly, against mere blind terror" (1:276–277). Exposure by the "straight" glare of the police is more tolerable than the terrible obliquity that has come to define relations in the novel. But in *The Golden Bowl*, policing has achieved a discretion that allows for neither overt recognitions nor protests.

Maggie also feels the appeal of a direct and spectacular vio-

6. The phrase is from Henry James, "The Jolly Corner" (1908), in *The American Novels and Stories of Henry James*, ed. F. O. Matthiessen (New York: Alfred A. Knopf, 1947), 810.

lence that would break in on the "simulated blindness" and "high decorum" (2:233) of the group. But the *pax Americana* that she arranges involves a radically different form of vigilance and correction. Maggie rehabilitates relations not through a violence that would people the scene with "shames and ruins" (2:235) but instead by instituting what I have called an *immanent* policing. The characters are perpetually "watching each other" (2:239), but Maggie, above all, "watched herself" (2:141) and gets the others to watch themselves, to adjust and to conform "autonomously" to the normative vision of the marriages that her power of mild insistence imposes. By the close of the novel, this vision is so deeply internalized in those she "treats" that it becomes questionable whether Maggie's surveillance can still go by that name, "if it now could be called watching" (2:358). The method of regulation that Maggie puts in place seems not like a discipline or supervision at all. At once insidious and irreproachable, Maggie disposes of a paradoxical power that consists of "systematic consideration" and "predetermined tenderness" (1:136), even as it constructs a prison cage of "bars richly gilt but firmly though discreetly planted" (2:230). Maggie's is a power of love, and her vigilance appears consistently as a "vigilance of 'care'" (1:325).

Criticism of *The Golden Bowl* has proceeded along two essentially incompatible lines, depending on whether the Ververs are seen as innocents or exploiters—on whether, that is, they are seen as characters of love or as characters of power. At the same time, however, criticism of the novel has at once acknowledged and repressed the virtual "interchangeability" of these characterizations. Thus, it has been argued that the novel presents a "strained and contorted fusion of what is authentic, normative, and good with what is false, perverted, and evil" (Holland) and, further, that "the terms 'good' and 'evil' in such a context lose their meaning, become interchangeable and, therefore, in an ultimate sense, 'absurd'" (Sears).[7] Whether readers of the novel

---

7. Laurence Bedwell Holland, *The Expense of Vision* (Princeton: Princeton

are of the Verver faction, of the anti-Verver faction, or of the "ambiguity" or even "absurdity" faction, what grounds all these readings is the notion of an absolute opposition between love and power. If *The Golden Bowl* has traditionally been regarded as the "large problem child among James's writings," as that other story of love and mastery, "The Turn of the Screw," has been read as "the small one," this is because the dominant tendency in this criticism, as in contemporary criticism of the novel generally, has been to keep these two terms—love and power—apart.[8] But I have begun to suggest that *The Golden Bowl* displays precisely a criminal continuity between these terms. Far from being opposed, love and power in *The Golden Bowl* are two ways of saying the same thing.

II

The opening passage of the novel poses the subject of power, but this passage proceeds precisely by disposing of, or better, displacing, this subject. The Prince, walking the London streets, reflects on the "question of an *Imperium*" and, more specifically, on the transfer of power from Rome to London: "He was one of the Modern Romans who find by the Thames a more convincing image of the truth of the ancient state than any they have left by the Tiber" (1:3). Such reflection, the narrator observes, might have "guided his steps" to one of the monumental sites of British power. But the Prince displays "no consistency of attention" and instead "strayed simply enough into Bond Street." He stops before a shop window and views "objects massive and lumpish, in silver and gold . . . , tumbled together as if, in the insolence of Empire, they had been the loot of far-off victories." Not merely

University Press, 1964), 374; Sallie Sears, *The Negative Imagination* (Ithaca: Cornell University Press, 1968), 222. For a useful listing of critical debate on the novel, see Ruth Bernard Yeazell, *Language and Knowledge in the Late Novels of Henry James* (Chicago: University of Chicago Press, 1976), 131–32.

    8. F. W. Dupee, *Henry James* (New York: Delta, 1965), 225.

does the narrative insist on the Prince's indirection; it also subscribes to that indirection. The superfluous "as if" divorces the effects of Empire from its causes. Such a "shuffl[ing] away [of] every link between consequence and cause" (2:345) marks, as we will see, the representation of power throughout the novel. But for now it may be noted that a further displacement of the subject of power immediately appears. The Prince again shifts his attention, this time from economic to sexual conquest, to the "idea of pursuit": considering the marriage arrangements then being negotiated, he observes that "capture had crowned the pursuit—or success, as he would otherwise have put it, had rewarded virtue" (1:4). Inconsequently drifting from imperial to economic to sexual questions, the Prince translates the terms of his marriage from "capture" and "pursuit" to "success" and "virtue," and the translation might be read as a final displacement—from his native idiom into American, the language of power in the novel: "He was practising his American in order to converse properly, on equal terms as it were, with Mr. Verver" (1:6).

If the novel thus begins by invoking the "real dimensions" (1:3) of power, the narrated displacement of power collates with a narrative power of displacement. On the one hand, the opening passage traces a distribution or dispersion of the political into economic, linguistic, and sexual relations; on the other, in its insistence on the discontinuity of the Prince's itinerary of concerns, the narrative treats these relations "as if" they were "simply enough" discontinuous with the subject of power. This is the double discourse that represents power in the novel: *The Golden Bowl* traces the dispersion of the political into the most ordinary and everyday relations, even as it shuffles away the links between power and its representations.

What the novel poses, then, is precisely a politics of representation. "Every one had need of one's power," Adam Verver reflects, "whereas one's own need, at the best, would have seemed to be but some trick for not communicating it" (1:131). If the first principle of the "vast modern machineries" (1:15) or technologies of power that traverse the novel is the *dispersion* of the political, what allows for this dissemination is this "trick" by which power never appears as such—the *recession* of signs of authority. Adam's power remains radically unlocatable within the novel. The only account that can be given of his "acquisitive power" (1:128) points to his "amiability," but James confesses, "the link . . . is none the less fatally missing" between the imputed cause and the "perfection of machinery" that is its effect (1:128). Power is the missing link in *The Golden Bowl,* and the narrative can present only negative evidence of Adam's mastery. "Deprived of the general prerogative of presence," "meagerness" and not "force" defines the billionaire's appearance—"so far as he consisted of an appearance at all" (1:169–170). Paradoxically, only this almost anonymous vacancy testifies to the "presence" of Adam's power: he seemed "so nearly like a little boy shyly entertaining in virtue of some imposed rank, that he *could* only be one of the powers, the representative of a force— quite as an infant king is the representative of a dynasty" (1:324). By this perverse logic, it is his childlike and almost infantile simplicity and innocence that become the only indices of Adam's potency. Adam represents power, but only by appearing powerless.

Clearly, the representation of mastery as a kind of radical innocence serves as an exemplary shelter for the exercising of power. "Power is tolerable only on condition that it mask a substantial part of itself," as Foucault has observed; "its success is proportional to its ability to hide its own mechanisms."[9] But if this strategy of recession is crucial to the ideology of power that James at once represents and, in his "making a mystery" of Adam, promotes, it also poses a threat to the success of that power. The danger inherent in Adam's trick of noncommunication is that "the effect of a reserve so merely, so meanly defensive [might] discredit the cause" (1:131).

The real threat, in other words, is that in appearing simple and

---

9. Michel Foucault, *The History of Sexuality,* trans. Robert Hurley (New York: Pantheon, 1978), 86.

innocent, Adam will be treated as if he were. Fanny indeed treats Adam "as if she were nursing a sick baby," and he "in irritation" "accused her of not taking him seriously" (1:137). More significantly, the image of Adam as a shy little boy is the Prince's, and this "generalized view" of his father-in-law supports a rather more serious instance of not taking Adam seriously. The view of Adam and Maggie as innocent, simple, and childlike constitutes the alibi for the Prince's intimacy with Charlotte. Protection of the happy innocents' "sweet simplicity" becomes the "conscious care" of the adulterers (1:311, 312). Their intimacy becomes a perverse way of "taking care of *them*" (1:309), a perverse but also "sincere" effort to "protect the father and the daughter" (1:310). This "complicated twist" in fact involves a complete if temporary *reversal* in the relations of power, a reversal premised on the very reserve of that power.

The revisions and rearrangements that make up the second book of *The Golden Bowl* are explicitly motivated by this discovery: the recognition that the exercising of power produces effects that exceed or even reverse the intentionalities of that power. In Foucauldian terms, where there is power, there are resistances. "From the moment the dear man married to ease his daughter off," Fanny explains, "it then happened by an extraordinary perversity that the very opposite effect was produced" (1:387–388). Every attempt to redress the balance of relations initially disrupted by Maggie's alliance with the Prince entails resistances and reverse effects that threaten the Ververs' conjugal accumulations and arrangements. And it is just this perverse overproductivity of attempts to fix and to control that generates the surplus of relations that jeopardizes the symmetry of the marriages and of the novel both. "She's no relation to you whatever," Fanny tells the Prince, referring to Charlotte, but what Fanny represses is the recognition that her own matchmaking—her making of the Prince's marriage and of Charlotte's "to make up for it"—has produced a relation. Or rather, as Maggie puts it, it has produced "*two* relations with Charlotte" or even "fifty": "It's of the number of *kinds* of relation with her that I speak" (2:190–191). The problem, as James comments in one of his prefaces, is that "relations stop nowhere," and this proliferation of alliances at once constitutes and destabilizes every ordering and fixing structure in the novel.

The very relational character of power exercises makes possible the formation of resistances: power can be "held" but not "owned" in *The Golden Bowl*. The general "rules"—dispersion, recession, and reversibility—that define the representation of power in the novel indicate that power cannot be conveniently localized or targeted; rather, power inheres in the structure of relations among characters, and this structure can always be rearranged. But for the moment I am more concerned with one further consequence of this strictly relational concept of power. If power is a relation, then every exercise of power is inevitably doubly binding. To arrange and to control is to enter into a relation with one's "adversary," and the bond thus formed is reciprocally coercive. Opponents are also counterparts, even partners. Alternatively, we might say that the novel brings into view what might be called the intimacy of power: adversaries are held together within what Maggie describes as the "steel hoop of an intimacy" (2:141). I now want to consider this continuity between power and intimacy: in what ways do the forms of intimacy in the novel—modes of protecting, taking care of, and loving—operate also as modes of policing and taking power?

III

Critics of the novel have debated whether Maggie triumphs through the creative force of a "sympathetic imagination" that affirms the "imaginative autonomy" of others or whether, on the contrary, she wins by "us[ing] her intelligence to control others," by denying "vital interchange with others."[10] But I have

---

10. Ruth Bernard Yeazell, *Language and Knowledge*, 113; John Carlos Rowe, *Henry Adams and Henry James: The Emergence of a Modern Consciousness* (Ithaca: Cornell University Press, 1976), 224.

already suggested that James insists on the interchangeability of these characterizations. Control and sympathy are not opposed here; in fact, Maggie controls precisely through a power of sympathy. Late in the novel, Maggie imagines her "place" among the marriages: "That place had come to show simply as that improvised 'post'—a post of the kind spoken of as advanced— with which she was to have found herself connected in the fashion of a settler or a trader in a new country; in the likeness even of some Indian squaw with a papoose on her back and barbarous bead-work to sell" (2:323–324). Maggie's place is clearly two places at once. But what appears as ambiguous or contradictory in this account of Maggie as at the same time the colonizing "settler" or "trader" and the colonized "squaw" is not, I want to argue, finally ambiguous or contradictory but rather the double surface of a single strategy. Maggie's empathetic improvisa- tions—her ability to put herself at once in the place of victim and in the place of victimizer—are the measure of her power. "I can't put myself into Maggie's skin" (1:311), Charlotte confesses, but it is just this ability to put oneself into another's skin that Maggie demonstrates.

Particularly interesting here is the manner in which Maggie's power of sympathetic identification inhabits a scenario of colo- nialism. In a provocative essay on the literature of the age of exploration, Stephen J. Greenblatt argues that the expansion of Western power can be closely identified with the emergence of a psychic capacity for "empathy," the "sympathetic appreciation of the situation of the other fellow." Resituating the claim of the social historian Daniel Lerner, in *The Passing of Traditional Soci- ety*, that Western society is defined by the enlightened and gen- erous ability "to see oneself in the other fellow's situation," Greenblatt shows the continuity between what Lerner calls the "spread of empathy around the world" and the spread of West- ern imperialism.[11] The psychic technique of mobility becomes

11. Stephen J. Greenblatt, "Improvisation and Power," in *Literature and Soci- ety: Selected Papers from the English Institute, 1978* (Baltimore: Johns Hopkins University Press, 1980), 57–58.

dominant with the political technologies of expansion; the ability to put oneself in the other's skin underwrites the infiltration and displacement of the other fellow, even as this colonization proceeds in the name of benevolence and sympathy.

It takes little interpretive pressure to see that the figure of Amerigo and his lineage, the allusions to Adam Verver's conquistadorial position on his "peak in Darien," make reference to the origins of Western imperialism and that Maggie's strained pax Britannica invokes the period of crisis of empire. Nor does it take much pressure to see that both cases involve an imperialism of sympathy and care. As J. A. Hobson observed in his *Imperialism: A Study* (1902), one of the traditional alibis for imperialism is the view of colonial expansion as a benevolent "mission of civilization."[12] There is perhaps some resemblance between the imperial civilizing mission, dispensing its "emissary of pity" to spread "wider sympathies" and operating "like a beacon on the road to better things . . . , humanizing, improving, instructing," and the great philanthropist's plan to erect a House of Civilization west of the Mississippi, "positively civilization condensed, concrete, consummate . . . , a house from whose open doors and windows, open to grateful, to thirsty millions, the higher, the highest knowledge would shine out to bless the land" (1:144). There is perhaps a resemblance, that is, between Conrad's representation of the improvised posts of the "great civilizing company" and Adam Verver's philanthropic "rifling of the Golden Isles" (1:141) to erect his temple of civilization in American City.[13]

I am suggesting that what operates on one level as a form of economic and cultural imperialism is discreetly reinvented on another, in the form of Maggie's domestic colonialism. On both

---

12. J. A. Hobson, *Imperialism: A Study*, rev. ed. (London: G. Allen, 1938), 16.

13. Joseph Conrad, "An Outpost of Progress" and "Heart of Darkness," in *Great Short Works of Joseph Conrad* (New York: Harper and Row, 1967). It is worth noting that James was preoccupied with the imperial crisis of the Boer War when he began work on *The Golden Bowl* and that the objet d'art that formed the model of the bowl itself was an imperial gift. See Leon Edel, *Henry James: The Master, 1901–1916* (New York: Avon, 1972), 63, 209.

surfaces, love and power mingle ceaselessly. Again, by wishing them well Maggie gets the others to do what she wants, and through her power of empathy she can put herself in the place of, and displace, her rival: by the close of the novel, the two had, simply enough, "changed places" (2:296). But Maggie's tactics of care by no means escape those resistances and reverse effects that are produced by every movement of control in the novel. The very ability that Maggie displays—her ability to stand in two places at once—indicates the instability of her own position. Furthermore, if Maggie proceeds against Charlotte by empathetically identifying with and "copying her companion" (2:13), if she attempts to rearrange relations by "turning the tables" (2:306) on her intimate opponents, she discovers that she herself has been copied and that the tables have already been turned on *her*. This reversal forces, at the start of the second book of the novel, Maggie's "first shock of complete perception" (2:45).

Through her "innocent economy" of love, Maggie has initially managed to place the Prince and Charlotte within her grand design. But she realizes, at the start of "her" book, that she herself has been excluded from the very "structure"—the "outlandish pagoda"—that she has constructed. Her own initiatives of arrangement have entrapped her within the situation that she herself has brought about. One might say of Maggie, as Charlotte says of Fanny, " 'She must stand exactly where everything has, by her own act, placed her . . . she's *fixed* . . . condemned to consistency' " (1:341). Maggie has begun to act—"she had flapped her little wings as a symbol of desired flight" (2:44)—only to discover that she has been immobilized by a counterstrategy of control and, moreover, by a strategy that has taken its "cue" from her own gentle way of supervision. It is by now perhaps not surprising that the counterplot that Maggie confronts consists of a "plan that was the exact counterpart of her own" (2:41), nor is it surprising that this plan involves a predetermined tenderness and systematic benevolence. Maggie finds herself imprisoned by an innocent economy that consistently imitates her own, enclosed in fact by a conspiratorial "intimacy of which the sovereign law would be the vigilance of 'care'" (1:325):

> It was a worked-out scheme for their not wounding her, for their behaving to her quite nobly. . . . They had built her in with their purpose—which was why, above her, a vault seemed more heavily to arch; so that she sat there in the solid chamber of her helplessness as in a bath of benevolence artfully prepared for her, over the brim of which she could just manage to see by stretching her neck. Baths of benevolence were very well, but at least, unless one were a patient of some sort, a nervous eccentric or a lost child, one usually wasn't so immersed save by one's request. [2:43–44]

It is tempting to say that this scheme of benevolence is merely a "cover" for what is after all a strategy of imprisonment. But such a reading would ignore Maggie's—and indeed James's—insistence on the sincerity and even nobility of the scheme. More pertinently, it would underestimate the real force of the plan and the larger significance of this startling incorporation of care and control. "They were *treating* her," Maggie discovers, and she becomes, in Jamesian terms, a subject for treatment through her immersion in a "bath of benevolence": she is, in the double sense that the narrative consistently exploits, taken care of. But the scandal here resides not merely in the fact that it is Maggie herself who "*began* the vicious circle" (1:394) that has come round to enclose her but also in that this is a vicious circle that hardly contains a vice. The real scandal of the perverse or "funny form" that the marriages have taken is that strategies of regulation and tender and "conscious care" are aligned not through some sort of mistake or deception or self-deception but because they are the same thing both times: "It's their mutual consideration, all round, that has made it the bottomless gulf; and they're really so embroiled but because, in their way, they've been so improbably *good*" (1:394). By the perverse logic of this embroilment, the mistake would be to imagine a way of disentangling this network of power and care.

The striking coherence of the benevolent scheme by which

Maggie is confined by Amerigo and Charlotte alerts her to *their* intimacy even as it reveals the terms of their relation to her: "She had become with them a subject of intimate study" (2:43). Maggie has been placed under watch and guard, has become at once a subject of knowledge and a subject of intimate and imprisoning vigilance. The nexus of knowledge, care, and regulation foregrounded here is perhaps clearest in the roles of "patient," "nervous eccentric," and "lost child" in which Maggie has been inserted. These roles recall the vision of Adam as a "sick infant" and small boy, a vision that, we have seen, sanctions the protective measures taken by the adulterers. Maggie's own treatment proceeds along the same lines, and the therapeutics that constitute it indicate the extent to which supervisory mechanisms have been embedded in procedures of caring, curing, instructing, and nurturing in the novel. Parent and child, doctor and patient, teacher and pupil—these are the roles occupied by characters in the novel, and this complex of roles defines the domain of power relations in *The Golden Bowl*.

The model for this network of relations is, not surprisingly, the *nursery*. More specifically, it is that "nursery of nurseries" (1:156) in which the Principino is both the nominal "master of the scene" and the subject of vigilant care. The site of the nursery makes explicit the innocent economy of care and supervision that characterizes all relations in the novel. James represents the nursery as a scene of power, a scene in which systematic consideration takes the form of a policing action. The doctor and nurse "mount unchallenged guard over the august little crib" (1:200), and if the child is nominally master, his guardian appears as the "true Executive." The double character of these roles—of guardianship and guarding—converts the nursery into a sort of benevolent prison. This politics of care makes it possible to speak of that "State, which began and ended with the Nursery" (1:202).

At one extreme, *The Golden Bowl* articulates its dismissal of the punitive and policing apparatus; but at another, the novel traces a widening of the orbit of this apparatus to include the most positive administrations of care. The world of *The Golden Bowl* is something like an extended nursery. This is perhaps clearest in the *tutelary* networks that penetrate virtually all relations in the novel. Fanny's "office" in the Verver household, for instance, is that of "common comforter" and "instructor." Both she and the Prince accept that "theory of their relation as attached pupil and kind instructress" (1:313). But this theory involves a tacit disavowal of the power play immanent in the relationship. Fanny's function, in relation to Amerigo, is "to keep him quiet," and she "limited indeed, she minimized, her office; you didn't need a jailer, she contended, for a domesticated lamb tied up with a pink ribbon. This wasn't an animal to be controlled—it was an animal to be, at the most, educated" (1:161).

Fanny, however, is mistaken on at least two counts: first, in her assumption that the Prince has already been "domesticated," and second, in her implicit opposition of the roles of the jailer and the educator. The second half of the novel involves precisely a process of *domestication,* and this process explicitly entails both a course of education, or reeducation, and an act of imprisonment. Indeed, if the Prince winds up "in his prison" (2:341), if his "pink ribbon" anticipates the "silken noose" (2:331) by which Charlotte is ultimately held in check, if Maggie's "general rectification" of the marriages resembles the construction of a "gilded cage," what this suggests is a rigorous continuity between tutelary, corrective, and disciplinary practices in the novel.

Characters in the novel are insistently engaged in "learning their lessons" (1:192, 205), in placing each other under surveillance as a "particular means of learning" (1:386). Adam's perverse courtship of Charlotte Stant invokes a rich cluster of therapeutic and remedial schemes: he proposes marriage as a cure, "remedy," and "service to his daughter" (1:208). But this courtship also centrally involves a "question of learning" (1:221); the desire to marry centers on what Charlotte later calls the "natural *desire to know*" (2:248, emphasis added). If Charlotte questions Adam's knowledge of her past, Adam converts this gap in knowledge into just the reason for this plan: "as strong a reason as I can want for just *learning* to know you" (1:221). All exchanges in the novel foreground this desire to know and the "teachability" (1:386) of the characters. They foreground as well the perfect "fit" between exchanges of knowledge and exchanges of power in the novel.

If "knowledge" in *The Golden Bowl* is both a "fascination and a fear," the reason is that the desire to know is also a will to power. Every gain of knowledge in the novel implies a correlative gain of power.[14] Fanny's "educative" relation to the Prince makes this explicit enough. The Prince, as Fanny recognizes, was "saving up . . . all the wisdom, all the answers to his questions, all the impressions and generalisations he gathered; putting them away and packing them down because he wanted his great gun to be loaded to the brim on the day he should decide to fire it off" (1:163). Knowledge in *The Golden Bowl* is, simply enough, a loaded gun. Further, since every transfer of knowledge is also inevitably a transfer of power, only when the Prince's "need of knowledge" has exhausted Fanny's supply is the convenient "theory" of their tutelary relation "quite exhausted." By the close of the first book, it is the Prince who "knows" and Fanny who has betrayed a certain "stupidity" (1:314), who lacks the means of learning, since the Prince has become "more closed than open to interpretation" (1:313). Lacking knowledge, Fanny is rendered powerless: "She doesn't understand us. . . . Fanny Assingham doesn't matter" (1:309).

But Maggie herself of course most richly displays this network of power and knowledge. Maggie achieves control simply by announcing *that* she "knows" and by refusing to tell *what* she knows. The formal and even theoretical purity of Maggie's position consists in her claim to possess "real knowledge" and her refusal to disclose its content; Maggie thus assumes a position of power without hazarding that power by putting her knowledge

---

14. See Leo Bersani, "The Subject of Power," *Diacritics* 7:3 (1977), 10, for a similar account of this power-knowledge network.

in exchange. Nothing could emphasize more the precise equivalence between knowledge and power in the novel than the
power of the term itself, "the effect of the word itself, her repeated distinct 'know,' 'know'" (2:200). Announcing that she
knows and remaining silent and discreet, Maggie virtually re-
cedes from view, and her power tactics here most clearly resemble her father's power of recession. Late in the novel, Maggie
observes the "trick" by which Adam controls Charlotte even as
he himself keeps "out of sight." "To have recognized, for all its
tenuity, the play of this gathered lasso might inevitably be to
wonder with what magic it was twisted," and recognizing the
magic trick by which Adam exercises power, Maggie's obser-
vance is also a means of learning, a lesson in power: "So many
things her father knew that she even yet didn't!" (2:331).

But before dealing with the way in which this tactic of regulation operates, I want to take up one final, and indeed, the central, case of tutelage in the novel. I have already noted the imitative character of the rivalry between Maggie and Charlotte,
the "copying" that marks their relation. This simulation makes
reference to the imitation implicit in all processes of learning. It
involves as well what René Girard has characterized as the imitative nature of desire.[15] The third term that completes the
circuit of power and knowledge in *The Golden Bowl* is love, those
movements of love and desire that traverse James's novel of
adultery.

At least one reader of *The Golden Bowl* has complained that the
"background" information that James gives us about his characters "remains unused": "The fact that Maggie and Charlotte
were school-fellows, for example, is never really brought to bear
on their relationship."[16] But the rivalry between Charlotte and
Maggie reinvokes this schooling relation with a startling explicit-

---

15. René Girard, *Deceit, Desire, and the Novel* (Baltimore: Johns Hopkins University Press, 1965). I am indebted to Walter Michaels for suggesting to me the
pertinence of a Girardian reading here.

16. Gabriel Pearson, "The novel to end all novels: *The Golden Bowl*," in *The Air
of Reality: New Essays on Henry James* (London: Metheun, 1972), 307. .

ness. Charlotte *"knows* the Prince. And Maggie doesn't," Fanny declares, provoking Bob Assingham's perversely apposite question: "So that Charlotte has come out to give her lessons?" (1:84). This transfer of knowledge—of the natural desire to know and of carnal knowledge—is precisely what takes place. Simply stated, Charlotte's intimacy with the Prince teaches Maggie how to desire him; Charlotte at once mediates and excites Maggie's own desire. Maggie's arrangements everywhere betray the necessity for mediators and surrogates in order for desire to be constituted, in Girard's terms, the "irresistible impulse to desire what Others desire, in other words to imitate the desires of others."[17]

It is not hard to recognize that Maggie acts by "promoting [the Prince's] interests with other women" and insistently arranges relations so that he is "being thrust, systematically, with another woman" (1:335). The sheer perversity of what is later called Maggie's "queer wish" is named in a passage that predicts the action of the novel's first book with an astonishing accuracy. One of the "easy certitudes" that characterizes the intimacy of Maggie and the Prince from the start

> was that she never admired him so much, or so found him heart-breakingly handsome, clever, irresistible . . . as when she saw other women reduced to the same passive pulp that had then begun, once for all, to constitute *her* substance . . . , she going so far as to put it that, even should he some day get drunk and beat her, the spectacle of him with hated rivals would, after no matter what extremity, always, for the sovereign charm of it, charm of it in itself and as the exhibition of him that most deeply moved her, suffice to bring her round. What would therefore be more open to him than to keep her in love with him? [1:165]

The fantasy or spectacle of the Prince's intimacy with a rival constitutes Maggie's desire, incites Maggie's own passion. Their love not merely permits but requires ("to keep her in love with him") these exhibitions. The Prince's relation, or two relations,

---

17. Girard, *Deceit, Desire, and the Novel*, 12.

with Charlotte are thus not simply a "flaw" in Maggie's design, but a necessary constituent of it: as Maggie observes late in the novel, it is "as if we had needed her, at her own cost, to build us up and start us" (2:346). It has recently been argued that adultery poses the threat of an "absolute annihilation of forms" in the nineteenth-century novel and that *The Golden Bowl* provides an "exemplary case" of the way in which the trangressive act of adultery "dissolves" the bourgeois form of marriage and the form of the bourgeois novel that centers on this institution.[18] But these forms, as we will see in a moment, are by no means so vulnerable to transgression and by no means so easily annihilated. Adultery, in *The Golden Bowl* at least, *constitutes* marriage.

Finally, these incitements to desire cannot be separated from the excitations of exercising power. When Maggie imagines the "steel hoop" that binds her to the Prince, she imagines "the steel hoop of an intimacy compared with which artless passion would have been but a beating of the air" (2:141). And if she fantasizes that the danger of defeat in her strategy of love "would hand her over to him bound hand and foot," if she feels the "new eagerness" of "working against an adversary" (2:142), what Maggie opposes to a merely "artless passion" is a passionate art of power. One must speak here, in Foucault's terms, of *"perpetual spirals of power and pleasure."*[19] One reader has recently suggested that "it is in the *moves* of desire that power slips," that the "geography of the fundamental passions" in which Maggie finally locates herself is, in effect, a world elsewhere.[20] But *The Golden Bowl* traces a criminal continuity between the movements of desire and the multiple deployments of power: it is in the moves of desire that this power takes hold.

This nexus of power and pleasure inscribes not merely Maggie's perverse lesson in intimacy but also all the relations of tutoring, caring, and loving that I have been tracing in the novel.

---

18. Tony Tanner, *Adultery in the Novel: Contract and Transgression* (Baltimore: Johns Hopkins University Press, 1979), 18, 86–87.

19. Foucault, *The History of Sexuality*, 45.

20. Bersani, "The Subject of Power," 21.

Seeing, knowing, and loving are bound up together in an intimate vigilance of care, and this vigilance involves both a fantasy of surveillance and the pleasures of knowing:

> The pleasure that comes of exercising a power that questions, monitors, watches, spies, searches out, palpates, brings to light . . . The power that lets itself be invaded by the pleasure it is pursuing . . . Capture and seduction, confrontation and mutual reinforcement: parents and children, adults and adolescents, educator and students, doctors and patients, the psychiatrist with his hysteric and his perverts, all have played this game continually since the nineteenth century.[21]

IV

If the story of this entanglement between loving and policing has been declared unreadable—confused or absurd—by readers of *The Golden Bowl*, it perhaps becomes readable, I have begun to indicate, as part of a story that social historians such as Foucault have recently started to narrate. At the close of *Surveiller et punir*, Foucault calls attention to the late nineteenth century's refinement of the "gentle way in punishment": the deployment of mechanisms of power that incorporate the "art of rectifying and the right to punish." I briefly sketched in the preceding chapter the gradual elaboration of a "power to punish [that] is not essentially different from that of curing and educating."[22] On somewhat different levels, historians such as Jacques Donzelot, Christopher Lasch, and Robert Castel have been defining the ways in which power relations have been progressively invested in agencies and institutions of rectification, cure, and pedagogy. We might speak here of the rise of the "helping professions" and "psy" sciences, of the expansion of state apparatuses of

---

21. Foucault, *The History of Sexuality*, 45.
22. Foucault, *Discipline and Punish* (New York: Pantheon, 1977), 303, 304.

health and education, of the general "medicalization" of modern Western society.[23]

The biography of the James family itself can serve as a convenient local instance of this general social reorganization of power around institutions of care and cure. The linkage of care and supervision is clear enough in Alice James's career as a professional invalid and, in a less emphatic way, in the invalidism of her brothers. The role of invalid, as Ruth Yeazell suggests, "always seems to have had its strange attractions for the Jameses."[24] Alice James's perverse vocation is virtually a map of late nineteenth-century therapeutic practices and also of the alliance of love and vigilance that these practices entailed.

If Alice resisted the "idiotizing" interventions of the medical "great man," her life was nevertheless centered on these inventions. As her biographer Jean Strouse relates, Alice James "brought extraordinarily high expectations to these encounters. In her family, the concern elicited by illness passed for love— and doctors were the scientifically sanctioned personification of solicitude and care."[25] Both Alice and Henry were familiar with S. Weir Mitchell's notorious "rest cure," an infantilizing therapy that immobilized the patient and subjected her to "entire rest" and to a minute supervision. And what indeed is Maggie Verver's imprisonment in a "bath of benevolence," as if she were some "nervous eccentric," but a displaced version of that cure?[26]

The professionalization of the medical sciences in the late

---

23. Jacques Donzelot, *The Policing of Families*, trans. Robert Hurley (New York: Pantheon, 1979); Christopher Lasch, *Haven in a Heartless World: The Family Besieged* (New York: Basic Books, 1977); Robert Castel, *L'ordre psychiatrique* (Paris: Editions de Minuit, 1977).

24. Ruth Bernard Yeazell, *The Death and Letters of Alice James* (Berkeley: University of California Press, 1981), 21.

25. Jean Strouse, *Alice James: A Biography* (Boston: Houghton Mifflin, 1980), 236.

26. Compare Jean Strouse, *Alice James*, 105–106. On Mitchell's rest cure, see Ann Douglas Wood, "The Fashionable Diseases," and Carroll Smith-Rosenberg, "Puberty to Menopause: The Cycle of Femininity in Nineteenth-Century America," both in *Clio's Consciousness Raised*, ed. Mary Hartman and Lois N. Banner (New York: Harper and Row, 1974), 1–37.

nineteenth century, and the collateral foregrounding of the figure of the doctor, form part of a complex redistribution of social
authority. Popular writers such as Havelock Ellis moved easily
from Lombrosian criminology to sexology to works on marriage,
diagnoses of the crisis of the family, of the "problem of the new
woman," hygiene, eugenics, eusthenics, domestic medicine, psy-
chiatry. These are new genres, opposed on part of their surface
but communicating on another level; they constitute a new discursive formation, what Jacques Donzelot has called the "medico-tutelary complex."[27]

This complex of disciplines invents and prescribes an array of
images and norms that effectively reforms social practices. Marriage and sexuality are spoken of in terms of apprenticeship,
skills, and an itinerary of goals set out by the counselors and
technicians of social relations. It becomes possible, for instance,
to speak of orgasm as an "achievement." Conjugality, the child,
and the family are progressively "supported" by what might
easily be called the Nursery-State. It becomes possible, in 1900,
to imagine that "a day will come when two families, before de-
ciding on a marriage, will meet with their two physicians in the
same way as they now meet with their notaries"—a proposal to
ensure racial purity that has come down to us as the required
premarital medical examination.[28] It becomes possible, finally,
to dream of a "federation of psychiatric republics where ordinary citizens would be examined, assembly-line fashion, from
the beginning of their main activities, by an army of prophylac-
tors, orientators great and small, sexologists of every stripe, specialists in suicide, head colds, automobile driving, and statistics."[29]

There is more involved here, however, than the steady expansion of the medico-tutelary complex. These moves to "federate"

---

27. Jacques Donzelot, *The Policing of Families*, 13–22 et passim.
28. Henry Cazalis, *La science et le mariage* (1900), as cited in Jacques Donzelot,
The Policing of Families, 185.
29. Gouriau, *Aliéniste français* (1932), as cited in Donzelot, *The Policing of Families*, 184.

and to professionalize everyday social practices promote new ways of viewing social transgressions and new techniques of discipline and correction. When Max Nordau, for instance, attacks the "degenerative" tendencies of fin-de-siècle culture, he explicitly draws on the nosologies of the criminal devised by Cesare Lombroso. But if Nordau sees the general movements in art and literature, of Zola and his school, for example, as essentially criminal, the point of view that he adopts is finally not that of the criminologist but rather the "clinical point of view." Nordau sets out the "symptoms," "diagnosis," and "etiology" of artistic degeneration, and ends his account by offering his "prognosis" and by prescribing a program of "therapeutics." Examining and classifying cultural hysterics, "graphomaniacs," and other "morbid deviations from the normal form," Nordau puts out a call for a "critical police," but he does not propose imprisonment. Rather, he recognizes that another form of institutionalization is already in place: "Our long and sorrowful wandering through the hospital—for as such we have recognized, if not all civilized humanity, at all events the upper stratum of the population . . . —is ended."[30] Nordau thus joins diagnosis and treatment in a single gesture: if modern society is diseased, it has already been hospitalized. If Bentham's Panopticon is the architectural model of the disciplinary society, the hospital is the centering site of the thoroughly medicalized society. And in this shift of social images and techniques one reads a mutation of the prison society of surveillance into a society comprehended and regulated by the clinical point of view, by the "vigilance of 'care.' " The medical examiner has become the examining magistrate of social norms and deviations.[31]

We have previously noted that even as Nordau attacks the illegality and criminality of the realist novelists, he compares their tactics of representation to those of the police report and thus implicitly points to the collaboration between the allegedly

---

30. Max Nordau, *Degeneration* (New York: Appleton, 1895), 536.
31. On the figure of the doctor-magistrate, see Michel Foucault, *The Birth of the Clinic* (New York: Vintage, 1975), 41–42.

criminal novelist and the regulative techniques of the law that I have traced in realist fiction. If Nordau here adopts the clinical gaze to condemn realist graphomania, it is nevertheless evident that this way of seeing is by no means outside the orbit of the realist novelist. Indeed, if I have readapted Zola's formula— "We novelists are the examining magistrates of men and their passions"—I have done so, in part, because Zola's program, as formulated in "The Experimental Novel," avowedly derives from the medical theorist Claude Bernard's *Introduction to the Study of Experimental Medicine.* As Zola simply puts the matter, "on all points I intend to fall back on Claude Bernard. Usually it will be sufficient for me to replace the word 'doctor' by the word 'novelist' in order to make my thought clear."[32] Nor is Zola's transposition of medical and literary terms at all anomalous. It is almost impossible to speak of the emergence of the realist novel and of its critical program without speaking of the emergence of the clinical point of view and of the medical and social discourses that constitute it. Flaubert, for instance, explicitly aligns the analytic perspective of the novelist with "le coup d'oeil médical de la vie."[33]

We might consider the frequent indictments of the realist text as a sort of dissection or vivisection of Taine's early career as a vivisectionist, physician writers like Chekhov or Holmes, the figure of the doctor in the novels of Flaubert, Turgenev, Eliot, and James. The list is familiar enough, and it indicates a crucial point of intersection between novelistic and clinical discourses. But I am less concerned here with the appearance of the topics of the physician and the clinical perspective in the realist novel than with a related but somewhat different question. To this point I have largely considered how relations in *The Golden Bowl* cohere around the movements of care, knowledge, and love promoted by the medical and tutelary complex. It is necessary now to ask

32. Emile Zola, "The Experimental Novel," in *Documents of Modern Literary Realism,* ed. George J. Becker (Princeton: Princeton University Press, 1962), 162.
33. Gustave Flaubert, *Oeuvres,* ed. Maurice Nadeau (Lausanne: Editions Rencontre, 1965), 6:260.

how this network of knowledge and care operates as a technology of regulation and, further, how the techniques of representation in the novel itself reinvent these techniques of control. The panoptic schema, it will be recalled, works not merely through a constant watchfulness but also by internalizing this watch in the prisoners themselves: the inmate is not merely watched, he watches himself. What is effected here, as Santayana noted, is a shift from "prohibition" to "compulsion." Furthermore, this system of compulsion is guaranteed by the formation of a normative scenario, a detailed grid of norms and deviations that effectively classifies and adjusts "morbid deviations from the normal form," intrinsically imposing forms of regularity and normality. This notion of the *norm* supplements and extends the rule of the law; and I want to suggest that the transition from the disciplinary to the clinical point of view forwards this move from the rule of the law and prohibition to the rule of the norm.

The concept of the norm is itself normative: one can hardly point out the difference between the normal and the abnormal, the correct and the perverse, without imposing a requirement of normalization and correction. The norm, as Georges Canguilhem observes in a provocative study of nineteenth-century medical concepts and their social application, is a "dynamic and polemical concept": the norm "increases the rule at the same time as it points it out."[34] The notion of the norm derives of course from the model of the organism and its power of self-regulation. The internal environment of the organism exists in a state of controlled equilibrium and maintains this equilibrium through constant regulative adjustments, or "homeostasis." The normal is achieved through a perpetual adjustment of deviations and abnormalities. Social programs of normalization effected during the course of the nineteenth century—in the institution of the prison, the factory, the school, the hospitals, and

---

34. Georges Canguilhem, *On the Normal and the Pathological* (Boston: D. Reidel, 1978), 146.

the family—aspired to this organic state of regulation or self-regulation. The goal is an immanent economy of power, internally and organically policed, an economy that ostensibly at least does not discipline or punish but rather "protects" and cares for "the health of the social body" and the relational equilibrium of its members.

Crucially, programs of normalization have the circular efficiency of the "normal school," a school in which teaching is taught. Always self-confirming, every deviation from the norm reaffirms the norm by providing an occasion for correction and normalization. As Canguilhem demonstrates, "it is not just the exception that proves the rule *as* rule, it is the infraction which provides it with the occasion to be rule by making rules."[35] The policing of the norm can scarcely be resisted, not merely because one can scarcely resist the normal, the healthy, and the correct, but also because the power of the norm not merely tolerates but requires resistances.

If Zola ratifies his method of representation by transposing the terms "doctor" and "novelist," it is by now perhaps clear that a related but more general transposition is possible here. What appears on the level of social and vital organization as a power of normalization reappears on the aesthetic as the rule of organic form. Or rather, we can point to the coemergence of these regulative concepts. Interestingly enough, the first use of the term "norm" (as recorded in the *Oxford English Dictionary*) is that of Coleridge in 1821; the first use of the term "normality" that of Poe in 1849: the aesthetics of organicism is an aesthetics of the norm. By the close of the century, the term "normalization" has appeared, and James has codified his "exceeding conviction that the art of fiction is an organic form."[36] James's organic principle of composition reinvokes point by point the analytics of power that I have been describing: the organic regulation of plot allows for a recession of narrative authority and makes for a dispersal

35. Ibid., 148.
36. R. P. Blackmur, Introduction to Henry James, *The Art of the Novel* (New York: Scribner's, 1934), xxiii.

of narrative control that is nonetheless immanent in every movement and gesture of character and plot. Moreover, for James
the rule of organic form provides a way of disavowing the violence of authorial manipulation and control even as regulation is
secured at every point in the narrative.

Above all, Jamesian organicism is a vigilance of care, a way of
knowing and controlling that James characteristically treats as
the "love" that the novelist has for his characters. James's clearest statement of this informing love occurs in his account of his
own literary tutelage, "The Lesson of Balzac." What is distinctive
about Balzac's novelistic practice, according to James, is his
method of "*penetrating* into a subject." This penetration is
achieved, in part, through Balzac's "inordinate passion for detail," his panoptic scrutiny of the figures he represents: "Every
mark and sign, outward and inward, that they possess." But
unlike Zola's "mechanical" saturation in information and detail,
Balzac's passion for detail penetrates because it is everywhere
informed by another sort of passion. Novelists, for James, are
preeminently "lovers of the image of life," and it is above all
Balzac's "love" of his characters that defines the "educative practice" of his fiction. This love expresses a "respect for the liberty
of the subject," a respect for and protection of the freedom and
autonomy of character: "The love, as we call it, the joy in their
communicated and exhibited movement, in their standing on
their feet and going of themselves and acting out their characters." The novelist refuses to interfere with or to "arrest" his
characters and resists the "'moral' eagerness" of judgment and
exposure. Rather, for the novelist who loves his character, "his
prompting was not to expose her; it could only be, on the contrary . . . , to cover her up and protect her, in the interest of her
special genius and freedom."[37]

But it becomes clear that this covering love covers for another
kind of exposure. The novelist's love of his characters is, in the

---

37. Henry James, *The Question of Our Speech; The Lesson of Balzac: Two Lectures*
(Boston: Houghton Mifflin, 1905), 85, 88, 72, 97–100.

sense we have considered, a colonizing empathy. Balzac, James writes, "loved the sense of another explored, assumed, assimilated identity," and this assimilative love is both a technique of control—"a love of each *seized* identity"—and a technique of knowledge: "It was by loving them . . . that he knew them." Finally, the very autonomy of the novelist's characters is merely a function of the virtually automatic mechanism of control and exposure in which they are inscribed. If the novelist's love of his character prompts him not to expose her, this exposure is nevertheless inevitable: it inheres in the "inner expansive force" of the form itself, in the "organic" rule of composition that is ultimately "the very law of the game." As if despite the novelist's covering love, over even the novelist's ostensible protests and regret, the character, of necessity, "is 'exposed,' so far as anything in life, or in art, may be, by the working out of the situation and the subject themselves; so that when they have done what they would, what they logically had to, with her, we are ready to take it from them." The organic "logic" of composition itself at last gives the character away. The shame of power is displaced upon the normalizing power of form, and if the novelist grants his character the freedom of "the long rope, for her acting herself out," this rope, completing James's figure, is finally the silken noose on which she hangs herself.[38]

In his preface to *The Golden Bowl,* James describes this double discourse of love and power in strikingly similar terms. "It's not that the muffled majesty of authorship doesn't here *ostensibly* reign; but I catch myself again shaking it off and disavowing the pretence of it while I get down into the arena and do my best to live and breathe and rub shoulders and converse with the . . . bleeding participants" (1:vi). Holding his "system fast . . . with one hand" while shaking off and disavowing authority with the other, the novelist proceeds as if the one hand did not know what the other was doing. This is the "embarrassed truth" that James at once confesses and covers: the radical entanglement

---

38. James, *The Lesson of Balzac,* 97–98, 107, 113, 99, 96.

between "their fortune and my own method," a method that has logically "foredoomed" the characters he loves (1:vi, vii).

But *The Golden Bowl* displays a power of normalization not merely in its form but also as the subject of its narrative action. The novel's second book, on both the level of composition and as the content of its action, brings to book the perversities produced by the first; and this general rectification of the monstrous and perverse is achieved through the power of the norm. Maggie's actions in the second half of the novel represent an almost diagrammatic institution of the rule of the norm. I have already noted that, in *The Golden Bowl*, it is the apparent "flaw" in Maggie's design—the deviation of adultery—that ultimately constitutes marriage. And this perverse deviation or infraction provides the occasion for Maggie's normalizing procedure. Again, the abnormal or exceptional reaffirms the norm, and the infraction empowers Maggie to reconstitute "the group normally constituted" (2:146). Maggie engineers a "conformity exquisitely calculated" (2:280), and the "terms of conformity" (1:334) that she imposes are of course the norms of the "happy family" and the "happy marriage" that she simply and consistently insists upon.

Maggie merely "floats" these images of the normative and good and invests the others, as she expresses it, with "something to conform to" (2:280). She allows relations to reestablish themselves in accordance with these images, to rearrange themselves as if autonomously, as if "the good moments . . . come round of themselves" (2:58). Crucially, these images specify at once a notion of *normal* relations and of *ideals* to be achieved. The norms of conjugal and familial relations deployed in the nineteenth century always operate, as Jacques Donzelot has observed, through such a "system of flotation"; the requirements of the norm (the implicit rule) and the normal (existing relations) are suspended in relation to each other, and the double nature of the norm—that which simply is and that which must be achieved—inherently promotes a movement of conformity.[39]

39. Donzelot, *The Policing of Families*, 211, 228–32.

We might alternatively say that what Maggie insists upon is "the golden bowl—as it *was* to have been" (2:216) and that she works to restore the ideal bowl, without a flaw, merely by repeating that it *is* and *always has been* what it was to have been. Maggie self-consciously and consistently floats the "standard of the house" (2:233), the something to conform to that normalizes relations: "Touch by touch she thus dropped into her husband's silence the truth about his good nature and his good manners; and . . . his virtue" (2:59). And through this conscious pretense, never deviating into the truth, this "truth" is finally established.

The self-regulative and almost tautological efficiency of Maggie's normalizing economy can hardly be overestimated. When Fanny protests against the "terror" of Maggie's way of making the others "do what I like," Maggie mildly appeals to the immanent rule of the norm. A punitive distinction between the correct and the deviant automatically enforces itself: "There wouldn't be any terror for them if they had nothing to hide" (2:116). Correction imposes itself only on that which requires correction; power is levied only on what resists it. The punishment does not merely "fit" the crime—the crime *is* the punishment. There is ultimately no escaping from the "penalty of wrong-doing" because the penalty is simply that one does wrong: as Maggie observes, a "foredoomed infelicity, partaking of the ridiculous even in one of the cleverest, might be of the very essence of the penalty of wrong-doing" (2:190). Perversity is the foredoomed penalty of the perverse.

But it would be a mistake to "personalize" this power of the norm, to locate it in Maggie herself. Rather, the self-rectifying and homeostatic rule of the norm resides in the imperatives of the organic structure to "right" itself, in what James in *The Golden Bowl* calls the law of the "equilibrium." "Their equilibrium was everything," Maggie recognizes, and the "sense for the equilibrium was what, between them all, had most power of insistence" (2:17, 39). If Maggie appears to be in control, this is because she has so thoroughly identified her desires with the requirements of the "precious equilibrium" itself: "She might have been for the time, in all her conscious person, the very form of the equilibrium they were, in their different ways, equally trying to save" (2:268). The power of the equilibrium operates so that in the "whirligig of time" things come round of themselves; it is the "form of the equilibrium" that guarantees the organic form of the action itself and ultimately "round[s] it thoroughly off" (2:340).

Thus what supports Maggie's strategy of rectification is the flexibility of the equilibrium: "The equilibrium, the precious condition, lasted in spite of rearrangement" (2:73). But it is just this capacity for rearrangement that has earlier made possible the turning of Maggie's original plan against her, and it is, I want to suggest, what makes possible one last reversal in the relations of power in the novel. If Maggie "for the time" seems to embody the very form of the equilibrium, her controlling love is, at the close, itself surrendered to a more comprehensive mechanism of control—to, in fact, what James in "The Lesson of Balzac" calls the "love" that the novelist bears for his characters: the love that logically and inevitably exposes through the organic working out of the situation itself.

We have earlier seen that *The Golden Bowl* persistently invokes the logic of cause and effect, even as it ostensibly severs the link between the "producing cause" (1:277) and its consequence. "The effect was nowhere in particular," the Prince, for instance, early considers, "yet he constantly felt himself at the mercy of the cause" (1:16). But if the narrative for a time has "shuffled away every link between consequence and cause," the inner and organic consistency of composition at last rejoins effects and causes. To the extent that the actions of James's late novels mirror the novelist's own compositional strategies, these actions are also caught up in the power play always implicit in James's organic and regulative principle of composition. Characters are subjected to, and even placed at the mercy of, the logic and "consistency" of the causal mechanism that, "sublimely consistent with itself" (1:357), ultimately seizes and exposes and seizes always in the name of love. If characters throughout the novel engage in struggles to keep from "giving themselves away"

(1:98; 2:115, 133), if they rearrange and "cover" themselves from exposure, they cannot finally resist the narrative logic that at last gives them away.

Appropriately enough, the closing reversal that I want to focus on involves a shift in power relations that is at the same time a shift in the trajectory of desire. The concluding paragraph of the novel has troubled readers of *The Golden Bowl,* not because that ending seems inconclusive, but rather because the terms by which closure is achieved have been considered radically ambiguous. The closing triumph of love incongruously appears as a tragic surrender. But what encourages this double reading of the ending is precisely that double discourse of love and power that, I have been arguing all along, structures the novel.

> It kept him before her therefore, taking in—or trying to—what she so wonderfully gave. He tried, too clearly, to please her—to meet her in her own way; but with the result only that, close to her, her face kept before him, his hands holding her shoulders, his whole act enclosing her, he presently echoed: "'See'? I see nothing but *you.*" And the truth of it had, with this force, after a moment, so strangely lighted his eyes that as for pity and dread of them she buried her own in his breast. [2:368–69]

The intimate reciprocity that the passage momentarily projects—the balance of taking and giving that culminates in the Prince's "echo" of the Princess's word—is a meeting of love that is also, for a moment, a balance of powers. But this balance is immediately breached through the Prince's very taking over of Maggie's terms. Seeing is never innocent in James's fiction, and to be seen and to be desired in *The Golden Bowl* is to be the object of power: the closing act of the novel is the Prince's own act of enclosure. Maggie's power is finally her "endless power of surrender" (2:352), and the "pity and dread" of her tragedy is a surrender and giving herself away to the "force" of the desire and the power that she has finally taught and transferred to the Prince.

There is more: Maggie's final surrender is also a surrender to the "predestined" law of exposure that the narrative invokes at its start. With a sublime consistency, the narrative rounds itself off by recuperating its beginning in its ending. Reinvoking the causes it has deferred, the narrative organically and inevitably enacts the movement of exposure that the Prince himself predicts at the very opening out of the drama:

> Once more, as a man conscious of having known many women, he could assist, as he would have called it, at the recurrent, the predestined phenomena, the thing always as certain as sunrise or the coming round of saints' days, *the doing by the woman of the thing that gave her away.* She did it, ever, inevitably, infallibly—she couldn't possibly not do it. It was her nature, it was her life, and the man could always expect it without lifting a finger. . . . She always dressed her act up, of course, she muffled and disguised and arranged it, showing in fact in these dissimulations a cleverness equal to but one thing in the world, equal to her abjection. . . . she was possessed by her doom. [1:49, 50, emphasis added]

V

Finally, if my reading of the criminal continuity between love and power in *The Golden Bowl* is correct, the traditional notion of the Jamesian novel, and of the aesthetics of the novel that it has been appropriated to support, must be thoroughly revised. In James's late fiction, love and power are two ways of saying the same thing, but criticism of *The Golden Bowl*, and of the novel generally, has worked not only to keep these two terms separate but to see them as absolutely contradictory. The novel is above all, in this criticism, the genre of love, a genre that resists and rejects the shame of power. "What I understand by an author's love for his characters," John Bayley writes in an influential study of the novel in general and of James in particular, "is a delight in their independent existence as *other people* . . . an intense interest in their personalities combined with a sort of detached solicitude, a respect for their freedom."[40] But the Jamesian solicitude for character is finally a vigilance of care, the respect for her freedom the long rope that immanently imposes her doom. "For James," John Carlos Rowe argues, "the artist is never an authority, but simply one who makes communication and dialogue possible."[41] But *The Golden Bowl* tells a different story, a story of power and authority told *as* a story of love.

Yet these readings perhaps represent more than a simple failure to read correctly. It is perhaps possible to claim that these misreadings have indeed learned the lesson that *The Golden Bowl* teaches. Every reading of the novel that enforces a distinction between love and power, every reading that treats the novel as the story of a rectification and "redemption" of the perverse and evil by the normative and good, every reading that recuperates the perverse entanglement of love and power in the novel as a triumph of love and of aesthetic form both might be said to repeat the very normalizing procedure that the novel itself at once names and secures. To rectify and to normalize, all in the name of love: this is to exercise power in the very act of disowning power, and it is this ideology of power that *The Golden Bowl* enacts and that these readings of the novel consistently reenact.

40. John Bayley, *The Characters of Love* (New York: Basic Books, 1960), 7–8.
41. Rowe, *Henry Adams and Henry James*, 217.

3

Advertising America:
The American Scene

> All life therefore comes back to the question of our
> speech, the medium through which we communicate
> with each other; for all life comes back to the question
> of our relations with each other. These relations are
> made possible, are registered, are verily constituted, by
> our speech.
> —JAMES, "The Question of Our Speech"

> In appearance, speech may well be of little account,
> but the prohibitions surrounding it soon reveal its
> links with desire and power. . . . speech is not merely
> the medium which manifests—or dissembles—desire; it
> is also the object of desire. Similarly, historians have
> constantly impressed upon us that speech is no mere
> verbalisation of conflicts and systems of domination,
> but that it is the very object of man's conflicts.
> —FOUCAULT, "The Order of Discourse"

I

"Modern sin takes its character from the mutualism of our time,"
the sociologist E. A. Ross declares at the start of *Sin and Society*
(1907), his popular critique of America's "sheer capitalism." By
"mutualism," Ross refers to the complex social and economic
"interdependence" that has come to characterize American society by the turn of the century; and this "webbed social life" has

produced, Ross argues, new and sinister possibilities of sin and crime: "wider interdependencies breed new treacheries." Ross charts the financial and civic corruptions and the "subtle iniquities that pulse along those viewless filaments of interrelation that bind us together." But the problem is just this nearly invisible, or "viewless," character of modern social relations and of the crimes it promotes. Not merely is the "reality of this close-knit life . . . not to be *seen* and *touched*," but as a consequence of this close binding, the criminal has become virtually indistinguishable from "us": "They want nothing more than we all want,—money, power, consideration." The criminal—or rather what Ross, following Lombroso, calls the "criminaloid" type—is a sort of "quasi-criminal" who practices a "protective mimicry" by which he "counterfeits the good citizen." Operating invisibly within a web of interdependencies and lacking the familiar "stigmata of the true criminal type," the modern criminal need only "press the button of a social mechanism" to effect a crime.[1]

Ross's difficulties in "drawing the line" between criminal and good citizen might have led him to conclude that the regime of American capitalism itself was criminal or criminaloid in character. But Ross insists that "the rules of the game are themselves sound" and argues instead that the problem lies in the invisibility of the new forms of social interrelation and the "blindness" that has allowed crime to go undetected. The solution that Ross proposes is, not surprisingly, a more effective way of seeing and detecting. If the criminal does not bear the "time-honored insignia of turpitude," if social complexity has allowed him to recede from view, a new technology of representation or "branding" must be invented "to put the soul of this pagan through a Bertillon system and set forth its marks of easy identification." Invoking the biometrics apparatus—a detailed grid of identifying signs—of the French statistician and criminologist, Ross dreams of a providential scrutiny of the soul. But paradoxically enough,

---

1. Edward Alsworth Ross, *Sin and Society: An Analysis of Latter-Day Iniquity* (Boston: Houghton Mifflin, 1907), 3, 6, 69, 34, 40, 51, 46, 59, 61–62, 28, 33.

this gridding of the soul can be accomplished only by instituting social defense mechanisms that extend the very networks of dependence and social machinery that have produced modern crime. "Social defense," Ross asserts, "is coming to be a matter for the expert," who alone can effect "intelligent social engineering." Hence we must "turn over the defense of society to professionals."[2]

Ross's account registers the coemergence of professionalism and social managerialism in the late nineteenth and early twentieth centuries in America. As the historian Thomas Haskell observes, in a recent study of the rise of professional social science in the United States, the "recognition of interdependence" reorients social thought and incites professionalizing movements in this period.[3] But most striking about Ross's account is that the interdependency that ostensibly poses a threat to social order at the same time underwrites the formation of more elaborate mechanisms of regulation. What appears from one point of view as a social crisis requiring the response of the expert appears from another as a rationale for a more intensive social vigilance and discipline. One is tempted to shift around the question that Ross poses: one is tempted to ask not how the rise of professional social engineering solves the problem of interdependence but rather what problem the "recognition" of interdependence solves.

It is not hard to see that the notion of the interrelatedness of social phenomena, as Christopher Lasch has noted, is a "commonplace truism" that effectively naturalizes the notion of an "invisible hand" that regulates industrial capitalism: "In modern society, relations among men appear to form a seamless web existing independent . . . of human volition. . . . In reality, this 'interdependence' merely reflects changing modes of domina-

---

2. Ross, *Sin and Society*, 27, 10, 50, 41, 42.

3. Thomas L. Haskell, *The Emergence of Professional Social Science* (Urbana: University of Illinois Press, 1977).

4. Christopher Lasch, *Haven in a Heartless World: The Family Besieged* (New York: Basic Books, 1977), 24.

tion."⁴ The notion of blindness works as a blind for the elaboration of new technologies of social control. Ross's representation
of modern crime, in the manner I have traced in the preceding
chapter, provides the occasion for the normalizing and managerial practices that begin to permeate American society in the late
nineteenth century. Society, in order to protect itself, must be
turned over to the engineering of professionals.

Although Ross's *Sin and Society* was appearing in the *Atlantic
Monthly* at the same time that James's *The American Scene* was
appearing serially in the *North American Review*, it may seem odd
or even impertinent to juxtapose these two representations of
turn-of-the-century America. James after all announces in his
preface that his subject will consist of "features of the human
scene . . . that the newspapers, reports, surveys and blue-books
would seem to confess themselves powerless to 'handle.' "⁵ The
novelist everywhere differentiates his account of the American
scene from the rival accounts of "the genealogist, the historian"
(p. 458) and disowns "the mere sharp shears of journalism," the
"loud statistical shout," the "ruins of the Language, in the
monthly magazines" and also the "black overscoring of science"
and the reduction of "*the* historic page" to the "mere bank-book"
(pp. 308, 297, 242, 75, 143). Against these "powerless" discourses James sets the "sovereign power of art" (p. 46). Disavowing the "political, the civic, the economic view," James's "aesthetic view" (pp. 55, 95) constitutes *The American Scene*.

James attempts to bring America to book by displacing these
alternate modes of representation, by radically opposing the
power of art to the discourses of power. But as I have already
begun to indicate, these ways of seeing impose themselves as
rival voices and as rival texts, competing with James's representational strategies and exerting a continuous pressure on them.
The "restless analyst" of *The American Scene* attributes "voices"
and "stories" to the sites, buildings, and cities that he seeks to

5. Henry James, *The American Scene* (Bloomington: Indiana University Press,
1968), xxvi (preface). Subsequent references to this edition appear in parentheses in the text.

interpret, and inscribing these voices into his text, James avowedly risks displacing his own narrative voice. The irruption of
these alien voices is similar, in fact, to the invasion of the aliens
themselves into America, an invasion that James presents primarily as a linguistic usurpation, as an encroaching "babble" of
"unintelligible" and "indecipherable" tongues that threaten to
"dispossess" him of a "living idiom" (pp. 122, 139). James's text
is traversed by a disparate array of voices, and its narrative line is
persistently dislocated and decentered by conflicting claims to
speech—by conflicting ways of composing and constituting
America.

But it is not merely that these discourses threaten James's art
of representation "from the outside." I have been arguing all
along that James's tactics of representation reproduce the very
tactics of power that he ostensibly resists and disowns. *The American Scene* is perhaps James's most comprehensive record of this
complicity. Critically assessing and explicitly rejecting the movements toward managerialism, professionalization, and social engineering that Ross, for instance, advocates, James's text, it will
be seen, holds out for the ratifying difference between the aesthetic view and the rival views that jeopardize it. Yet throughout,
James notes the "democratic consistency," the "underlying unity," the "immense promiscuity" (pp. 55, 117, 103) that characterize America and that pose the danger of an indifferent
"merging" and "effacement of the difference" (p. 167). What
Ross calls mutualism or interdependence James calls "criminal
continuity," and I want to suggest that James's analysis of the
American scene reveals precisely an underlying unity and continuity between art and power.

In fact, the very competition among modes of discourse that
James represents—the partitioning of political, economic, and
aesthetic views—internally registers this continuity even in the
act of denying it. We find here what Mikhail Bakhtin has called a
"professional stratification of languages," a stratification that involves not only the languages of business, law, politics, medicine
but also the language of literature itself: as Bakhtin observes,

"the very language of the writer (the poet or novelist) can be taken as a professional jargon on a par with professional jargons."[6] *The American Scene*, and also the prefaces to the New York Edition that James wrote soon after his return from his American tour, clearly constitute a movement of literary professionalization: a formalizing of the aesthetic view and of the art of the novel, the codification of an ensemble of techniques and critical procedures, the emergence of the writer and critic as expert. *The American Scene* confronts this "whole subject of expertness" (p. 399), and even as James resists the society of professionalism, his own aesthetic views and techniques reinvent the very technologies of that society. This double gesture of resistance and complicity, played out primarily as a competition among discourses, is what I want to investigate in *The American Scene*, and what I shall suggest is that James's text reveals finally not an opposition between art and power but, indeed, an *art of power*.

II

One way of clarifying the terms of this competition is by contrasting James's policies of representation in *The American Scene* with H. G. Wells's rather different account in *The Future in America* (1906), also written as James's work was appearing serially and often reading as an ironic commentary on his "illustrious predecessor's" version of America.[7] Wells celebrates the vast literature of "exposure" and "self-examination" that began proliferating in America in the last decade of the nineteenth century, making reference, for instance, to Riis's *How the Other Half Lives*, Steffens's *Shame of the Cities*, Lawson's *Frenzied Finance*,

---

6. M. M. Bakhtin, *The Dialogic Imagination*, ed. Michael Holquist (Austin: University of Texas Press, 1981), 289.

7. H. G. Wells, *The Future in America: A Search after Realities* (New York: Harper, 1906), 5. Subsequent references to this edition appear in parentheses in the text.

Tarbell's *History of the Standard Oil Company,* and Veblen's *Theory of the Leisure Class.* For Wells, this literature represents a "large collective process": "We work in shoals," he observes, "we are getting the world presented . . . , we build together" (p. 208). It is, indeed, the inscription and projection of America "by committee" that Wells promotes, and he sees these texts as a productive force, contributing to, and even constituting, America's future.

Wells also notes that he has been "reading, instalment by instalment, the subtle fine renderings of America revisited by Mr. Henry James" (p. 256). But Wells sees *The American Scene* as little more than an eccentric digression from the productive and scientific analyses offered by other examiners of the American situation. As Peter Conrad has recently suggested, Wells implies that "James has wished his own ineffectualness on America, decoratively describing the social fancies not the social and economic substance of the country."[8] It is not hard to see how James's text deviates from the other accounts of America that Wells invokes. The novelist's "confessedly subjective" account (p. 306) self-consciously "snap[s] its fingers at warrants and documents" (p. 308), and the "hard little facts" of social and economic life are insistently displaced by the "great soft fact" (pp. 336, 337) of the aesthetic view. Indeed, James from the start confesses that these rival representations, these "prodigious reports and statistics," record a "thousand matters" about which he finds himself "incapable of information" (p. xxvi).

The measure of James's "incapacity" is perhaps taken by Wells in his comments on Washington society, comments that register also a clear critique of James's tactics of representation. "There was, I found, a little breeze of satisfaction fluttering the Washington atmosphere," Wells remarks:

> Mr. Henry James came through the States last year, distributing

---

8. Peter Conrad, *Imagining America* (New York: Oxford University Press, 1980), 133.

epithets among their cities with the justest aptitude. Washington was the "City of Conversation"; and she was pleasantly conscious that she merited this friendly coronation. Washington, indeed, converses well, without awkwardness, without chatterings, kindly, watchful, agreeably witty. She lulled and tamed my purpose to ask about primary things, to discuss large questions. . . . Washington remarked and alluded and made her point and got away. [p. 240]

If James distributes epithets with aptitude, his activity is ironized in Wells's association of that activity with the fluttering of a "little breeze," and the easy transition from James's verbal act of coronation to Washington conversation reductively situates James within the evasive medium of that conversation. Wells aligns James's discourse and Washington conversation, equates their elision of "primary things," their habits of allusion and evasion, their substitution of small talk for "large questions." Wells, here and elsewhere, objects to James's "get-away" tactics, a tactics of evasion that talks past the hard social facts Wells takes as "primary."

It is precisely, I will be arguing, James's examination of the entanglement between discourse and the exercising of power in the "City of Conversation" that centers his reading of the "*vox Americana*" in *The American Scene*.[9] But my intent here is not to explain away James's evasion of those facts of power that Wells, and more recent critics of James's text, have seen him as censoring from his account of America.[10] Rather, this tactic of evasion is everywhere acknowledged in *The American Scene*. The Jamesian policy of representation avows its affinity with what James calls "our ineradicable Anglo-Saxon policy, or our seemingly deep-seated necessity, of keeping, where 'representation' is concerned, so far away from the truth and the facts of life as really to betray a fear in us of possibly doing something like them

---

9. James, *The Question of Our Speech; The Lesson of Balzac: Two Lectures* (Boston: Houghton Mifflin, 1905), 35.
10. See especially Maxwell Geismar, *Henry James and the Jacobites* (New York: Hill and Wang, 1965), 338–54.

should we be caught nearer" (p. 198). James both exposes and complies with this "necessity," and the art of representation in *The American Scene* advertises itself *as* an art of evasion. Obtrusively cultivating a "felicity of suppression and omission," James presents himself as habitually yielding to "the impulse irresponsibly to escape" from the "truth" and engages in what he describes as an "artful evasion of the actual" (pp. 204, 130, 87).

But James's willingness to risk and to advertise this art of evasion is perhaps somewhat too self-evident, and the counterexample of Wells's *The Future in America* can perhaps make clearer what lies behind James's discursive policy. Wells, I have indicated, views the investigation and projection of America's future as a "collective" process. His emphasis on documentary collaboration corresponds to the sort of future that Wells envisions. The bywords of Wells's account are "order," "organization," and "discipline," and he advocates, on every level, the "constant substitution of larger, cleaner, more efficient possibilities, and more and more wholesale . . . methods of organization for the dark, confused, untidy individualistic expedients of the Victorian time" (p. 86). A "common ordered intention" must be instituted to govern America's future, a future that consists of the ongoing conversion of a "moblike rush of individualistic undertakings into a planned and ordered progress" (p. 52). Wells projects the promise of an efficiently planned and managed society: the America of the future will be "electrical and scientific, artistic and creative" (p. 86).

Crucially, for Wells, the scientific and artistic views are not opposed but equivalent. For the writer of science fiction, "science is the 'equal sign' between the real and the imaginary. Its power is thus essentially poetic."[11] This equation, at a single stroke, undoes James's distinction between the actual and the aesthetic. James insistently opposes the imaginative liberty of the literary, and more particularly, as we will see in a moment, the

---

11. Pierre Macherey, *A Theory of Literary Production*, trans. Geoffrey Wall (London: Routledge, 1978), 169.

freedom of the literary romance, to the constraining laws of economic and scientific fact. James opposes the aesthetic techniques of the romance to the technologies of a certain scientific realism in his attempt to evade and to exceed the actual. But science here achieves just this romantic outstripping of the real: science is the technology of romance. Wells, it might be said, literalizes the Jamesian assertion of the sovereign power of art even as he reverses the force of this assertion, even as he effaces the distinction between art and power that James advertises and works to protect.

There is more to be said about this startling merger of the real and the imaginary and about the danger that it poses for James's attempt to imagine an alternative to the facts of power. For now, it may be noted that Wells's equation of the scientific and artistic implies not merely a poetics of technology but also the dream of a social order created and supervised by the laws of scientific management. Wells's account of the future in America is backed by the comprehensive social redistribution of power that has been characterized as the formation of the "age of organization" and, more recently, as the institution of the panoptic or "disciplinary society."[12] The deployment of a managerial mode of social organization is represented diversely by Ross's call for massive social engineering, by Frederick Winslow Taylor's formulation of a code of industrial efficiency in his *Principles of Scientific Management* (1911), and by the establishment of the centrally administered "model" town at Pullman, Illinois, in 1880, a company town "in which every movement was calculated to impress Americans with spatial order, cause and effect, efficiency, and a superintelligence."[13]

On a somewhat different level, the techniques of social panopticism ground Edward Bellamy's vision, in his utopian novel

12. Sheldon Wolin, "The Age of Organization and the Sublimation of Politics," *Politics and Vision* (Boston: Little, Brown, 1960); Michel Foucault, *Discipline and Punish: The Birth of the Prison*, trans. Alan Sheridan (New York: Pantheon, 1977).

13. Burton J. Bledstein, *The Culture of Professionalism* (New York: Norton, 1976), 74.

Looking Backward (1888), of a future America that has projected
military methods of discipline and hierarchical supervision onto
industrial and social organization. Bellamy's utopia is a disciplinary utopia, supported by an "industrial army" and regulated
through "vast economies effected by concentration of management and unity of organization."[14] This "perfectly organized"
America is inscribed by rigorous mechanisms and "stringent discipline" and is policed by a "systematic and constant oversight
and inspection." Supervision is immanently effected through a
massive "system, which in a great concern does the work of the
master's eye in a small business."[15] Fourier's Phalanstery has
taken on the form of Bentham's Panopticon: a utopia functioning under the mastering eye of a rationalized system of management, Bellamy's America employs the exemplary conjunction of
seeing and power that defines the panoptic technology.

More generally, this disciplinary matrix appears in a micropolitics of efficiency, normalization, and social engineering that
penetrates all areas of American life. I refer to the comprehensive reordering and partitioning of space, time, and words that
takes off in late nineteenth-century America: the formation of
the academic and administrative "disciplines," the elaboration,
as we have already noted, of a "culture of professionalism," with
its techniques of hierarchization, classification, and specializa-
tion, the centering of "truth" on the forms of scientific discourse
and on the institutions that produce it.[16] These disciplinary
functions spread throughout the social body, progressively re-
organizing both the great apparatuses of power and knowledge
and the forms of everyday life.

As Frederick Taylor suggested, "The fundamental principles
of scientific management are applicable to all kinds of human

---

14. Edward Bellamy, *Looking Backward: 2000–1887* (1888; reprint ed., New
York: Signet, 1960), 143, 53.
15. Bellamy, *Looking Backward*, 61, 134, 55.
16. See, for instance: Bledstein, *The Culture of Professionalism;* Haskell, *The
Emergence of Professional Social Science;* Michel Foucault, *Power/Knowledge,* ed.
Colin Gordon (New York: Pantheon, 1980), 118–33.

activities, from our simplest individual acts to the work of our great corporations."[17] Thus, Henry Ward Beecher could anticipate Taylorism in his insistence on the "science of management" entailed by a "science of preaching," and Thorstein Veblen could extend the normative criteria of economy and efficiency, in his critique of "waste" in the leisure class, to speech itself: "purity of speech," Veblen simply states at the close of *The Theory of the Leisure Class* (1899), argues "waste of time and exemption from the use and the need of direct and forcible speech."[18] Not merely are the institutions of the factory, the hospital, the school, the family rewritten, but also the institutions and orders of discourse; and, in a circular process, the formation of new discourses multiplies the effects of the disciplinary power that sponsors these discourses.

The American Scene proceeds by invoking this disciplinary scenario and the discourses that promote it. Moving through America, James reports, "One had perhaps never yet seemed so to move through a vast simplified scheme" (p. 305). The simplification is accomplished by the American "genius for organization" (p. 106), and this organizing genius effects its simplification—its "prompt reducibility of a thousand figures to a common denominator" (p. 452)—through a rigorous exclusion of deviations from the norm. James everywhere encounters the "jealous cultivation of the common mean, the common mean only, the reduction of everything to an average of decent suitability" (p. 442). The system operates to exclude any "happy deviations from the regular" (p. 243), and the order instituted is excessively, even tautologically, coherent. The restored absentee is subjected to a "severe discipline" enforced by the universal "combination of such general manners and such general prices, of such general prices and such general manners" (p. 235). If the New York skyscrapers represent for Wells the first installment of a "shining

17. F. W. Taylor, *The Principles of Scientific Management* (1911; reprint ed., New York: Norton, 1967), 7.

18. Thorstein Veblen, *The Theory of the Leisure Class* (1899; reprint ed., New York: Modern Library, 1934), 399–400.

order, of everything taller, wider, cleaner, better," they are for James emblems of America's simplified and sanitized regularity—"the horrific glazed perpendiculars of the future" (p. 228).[19]

What James opposes to the American achievement of normality and regularity is a deviant art of evasion. If the "eternal American note" is the "note of the gregarious, the concentric," James sets against this generalizing and centralizing force the "rank eccentricity" of his text (pp. 71, 450). Insistently exploiting the "opportunity of any deviation, in other words, into the *un*common" (p. 45), the style of *The American Scene* is explicitly a style of deviation. Resisting those discourses that have inscribed on the "American street-page" a "merely rectangular criticism" (pp. 244, 227), James cultivates a stylistic excess that evades the norm and strays into "margin, over-flow, and by-play" (p. 45).

If the American scheme marginalizes or even excludes the aesthetic view, James thus converts this exclusion into the first principle of his aesthetic, embracing the antinomy between aesthetic and political views. Critics of *The American Scene*, following the route that James has so clearly marked, have repeated this break between stylistic preoccupations and historical or political claims. Thus, Peter Buitenhuis remarks that James's "simplified view of the historical process is a limitation of the book. From an artistic point of view, however, it is an invaluable unifying force."[20] The discontinuity between artistic and referential imperatives could not be more clearly stated, and the critical tendency, here and elsewhere, has been to divert attention from James's ostensible subject to his techniques of representation and to convert matters of reference to matters of self-reference. Hence it is maintained that "the pilgrimage of the artist is made in his creative activity. . . . the real story is that of the analyst" (Rowe), that *The American Scene* is really "about its own composition and its own composer . . . , *is* in reality . . . personal auto-

---

19. Wells, *The Future in America*, 43.
20. Peter Buitenhuis, *The Grasping Imagination: The American Writings of Henry James* (Toronto: University of Toronto Press, 1970), 188.

biography" (Taylor).[21] It does not finally matter whether this break between subject and treatment is read negatively, as a retreat to the merely "literary" (as Wells, and more recently Geismar, have read it), or positively, as the triumph of the artist over "the formless and often chaotic world he encounters."[22] Either way, aesthetic and worldly claims are antithetical: the scene of *The American Scene* is really the scene of composition.

I have begun to indicate, however, the entanglement between compositional and historical, discursive and political practices. The scandal of *The American Scene* would seem to be James's artful evasion or disavowal of the actualities of history and power. What I have provisionally suggested is that James risks, and even calls attention to, this scandal in order to repress what is truly scandalous about his text: not an opposition between art and power but an underlying unity and discreet continuity between them. Having sketched in general terms the networks of power that traverse the American scene and the tactics of resistance that James devises to evade them, I now want to define the terms of this collaboration by examining three exemplary sites of power in *The American Scene:* the world of the hotel, the corrupt Quaker city, and Washington, the city of conversation and power.

III

The economist Richard T. Ely, describing the systematically and centrally administered company town at Pullman, Illinois, observed that living at Pullman was "like living at a great hotel."[23]

21. John Carlos Rowe, *Henry Adams and Henry James: The Emergence of a Modern Consciousness* (Ithaca: Cornell University Press, 1976), 164; Gordon O. Taylor, "Chapters of Experience: *The American Scene,*" *Genre* 12:1 (Spring 1979), 95, 115.

22. Geismar, *Henry James and the Jacobites,* 338–54; Rowe, *Henry Adams and Henry James,* 158.

23. Richard T. Ely, "Pullman: A Social Study," *Harper's New Monthly Magazine* 70 (February 1885), 452–66; see also Stanley Buder, *Pullman: An Experiment in Industrial Order and Community Planning, 1880–1930* (New York: Oxford University Press, 1967).

Both Pullman and its product—the railway "hotel-car" that transports James across America—testify to the force of what James calls the "hotel-spirit" in America: that combination of the "perpetually provisional" (p. 408) and the "universal organizing passion" (p. 445) that he finds everywhere inscribed on the American scene. James reads the "note of the hotel, and of the hotel-like chain of Pullman cars, as the supreme social expression" of the emergent American scheme, as the "great symbolic agent" of America's future (pp. 406, 465). The hotel-world and the hotel-spirit figure for James throughout as metonyms of the new American society.

James suggests that the hotel-spirit might "just *be* the American spirit most seeking and most finding itself" (p. 102), and this reciprocity of seeking and finding makes reference to the most visible achievement of the hotel-world: its perfectly self-contained order and equilibrium. The world of the hotel appears above all as a "social order in positively stable equilibrium" (p. 105) and functions as an absolutely self-enclosed and self-sufficient society, possessing a "complete scheme of life" (p. 102). This impressive order and equilibrium, this excessive and even tautological coherence and stability, represent an "ideal" of social relations. They ideally define as well a certain power relation.

The order of "hotel-civilization" (p. 438) is characterized by a beguiling luxury and harmonious revelry. Behind the visible harmony and equilibrium of this little world lies a discreet and comprehensive system of management. The revel is, James observes, "prescribed" (p. 438). If the hotel-world seems to operate through a virtually self-regulating economy, it is in fact governed by the invisible hand of the "master-spirits of management" (p. 106), a mastering spirit that exercises an immanent and diffused power of administration "whose influence was as the very air" (p. 106). The "testimony" of the hotel is a testimony to absolute managerialism: it is a world "organized with the authority with which the American genius for organization . . . alone could organize it" (p. 105). The domain of the hotel is not merely entered but administered—"I say with intention 'administered'" (p. 99)—and as the amazing hotel-world "closes round him" (p. 102), James finds himself captured and enclosed by the "omniscient genius" of the hotel-spirit (p. 439). If the hotel-world provides a glimpse of "perfect human felicity," it is also a "caged world (p. 441). Elaborately and tactfully organized, it is characterized by an "element of ingenuous joy below and of consummate management above" (p. 105). This "joy" is constituted by the regulative rule of the norm. The hotel's economy of equilibrium is achieved through a thorough suppression of excess and deviation, through a complete elimination of desires not prescribed and gratified by the closed order of life dictated by the hotel-spirit itself. Thus, James notes the "general machinery" that keeps down the appearance of "desired adventure" and the policies of management that enforce a "reduction of everything to an average of decent suitability" (p. 442). The caged world in effect imposes a normative grid on its inhabitants. Regulating and compressing all under "one vast cover" (p. 449), the managerial spirit produces a "neutrality of respectability . . . against which any experimental deviation from the bourgeois would have dashed itself in vain" (p. 455).

The master spirits of organization exercise an almost providential supervision over the movements of the caged populace, and the balanced economy of the hotel-world is so complete that it incorporates even a scheme of salvation. The "achieved harmonies" (p. 105) of the Waldorf-Astoria, for instance, were "both its earth and its heaven" (p. 104), and the two great hotels that James enters in Florida are a "divine Pair" (p. 447). To pass through their "high gates and gilded, transparent barriers" is to be enclosed within a "costly reproduction" of heaven itself, a heaven of exquisite conformity that admits only those who have duly submitted to the norms of hotel civilization: "To some such heaven, some such public exaltation of the Blest, those who have conformed with due earnestness to the hotel-spirit . . . may hope eventually to penetrate or perhaps actually retire" (p. 447). A paradise characterized at once by a perfect happiness and by a comprehensive supervision and confinement, the hotel is perhaps the ultimate realization of the panoptic ideal. A prison that resembles a paradise, the gilded enclosure makes and imposes its law: "The whole housed populace move as in mild and consenting suspicion of its captured and governed state . . . , beguiled and caged, positively thankful, in its vast vacancy, for the sense and the definite horizon of a cage" (p. 441).

The power exercised by the masters of organization is at once omnipresent and tactfully kept out of view; everywhere immanent, power is nowhere to be seen. Inscribed within the scene that he is representing, James reenacts this nexus of power and discretion, and his reenactment is so effective that critics of *The American Scene* have been led to argue that the hotel is, in fact, not the exemplary site of power and control but instead a refuge from the violence of power. Thus, one of James's most perceptive readers, Laurence Holland, suggests that James finds the Waldorf-Astoria a "welcome refuge from the 'inconceivably bourgeois' constrictions of the city's grid plan . . . and the 'violence' generated by its intersections." The violence, Holland continues, "extended even to the threshold of the hotel, but once projected inside James finds an oasis of socialized activity."[24] But the hotel-world, as I have indicated, provides not a refuge from but a continuation of this constriction and this violence. A bourgeois "grid" of a more insidious and more effective sort regulates this world and its caged populace. The "violence outside" is expertly dissimulated and dissembled. The hotel-world is held together by a "violence which all its warmth, its colour and glitter so completely muffle" (p. 100). This "warmth," "colour," and "glitter" make up what James calls the "art" of the hotel-spirit, and it is this art that muffles the violence of the hotel-world and covers its power of management.

If the hotel sphere is a panoptic environment, it is an aesthetic

24. Laurence Holland, "Representation and Renewal in Henry James's *The American Scene*," Appendix to his *The Expense of Vision* (Baltimore: Johns Hopkins University Press, 1982), 425.

panopticon. It expresses both a social and "indeed positively an aesthetic ideal" (p. 102). In one sense, the hotel aesthetic involves merely the vulgar "riot of creation" (p. 440). The "gilded and storied labyrinth" (p. 105) of the Waldorf-Astoria, with its "costliest reproductions" (p. 447) and "pretended majesties" (p. 103) is a product of the imitative art of the Gilded Age.[25] The hotel appears as a "play-house of the richest rococo" (p. 106) in which "art and history" are imitated and counterfeited. It is a theater in which the "play of the genius for organization" is expensively and profitably staged (p. 106). One of George Pullman's dicta, as Ely relates, concerned the "commercial uses of beauty," and the hotel spirit capitalizes on an "inordinate desire for taste" and appears as an earlier version of what the Frankfurt school theorists called the "culture industry." Exploiting this desire, the "great national ignorance of many things is artfully and benevolently practiced upon" (p. 440).

But the interlacing of art and power in the hotel-world is not limited to the commercial exploitation of an ignorant desire for taste. Beyond this explicit and local appropriation, there is an aesthetic ideal that appears in a less obvious and more significant form, in a form that threatens to compromise James's own art of representation. If James reenacts the policies of the hotel-world, this world reiterates and reenacts his own policies of aesthetic form. The perfectly stable equilibrium of the hotel is also a model of perfect formal economy and organic unity. The hotel is "absolutely a fit to its conditions" (p. 104), and every element of the exhibition "was on the best terms with all the rest." It is a complex composition "exempt from any principle or possibility of disaccord with itself." Incorporating the normative and the organic, the hotel is a triumph of form, of the Jamesian imperative of organic regulation; and, indeed, James twice confesses to an "ache of envy" (p. 104) as he views this achievement of the "technical imagination" (p. 107).

25. See, for instance: James Remington McCarthy, *Peacock Alley: The Romance of the Waldorf-Astoria* (New York: Harper, 1931); Lewis Mumford, *The Brown Decades: A Study of the Arts of America, 1865–1895* (New York: Dover, 1955).

It has been argued that "the America to which James returned seemed one possessed by that business imagination which the novelist's own imagination had rejected."[26] But the art of *The American Scene* represents not a "sublime economy" that transcends the vulgar economy of capitalist organization but rather a "desperate economy" (pp. 358, 429), and this desperation registers the precise equivalence between the economy of form and the economy of power. The omniscient genius of the hotel-world exercises a consummate control over his "material" and subjects. This managerial spirit appears as "some high-stationed orchestral leader, the absolute presiding power . . . , controlling and commanding the whole volume of sound, keeping the whole effect together and making it what it is" (pp. 106–107). Like the novelist whose narrative authority is at once omniscient and immanent, the presiding power exerts a comprehensive supervision over his characters while perpetuating the ruse of their freedom: he controls "an army of puppets whose strings the wealth of his technical imagination teaches him innumerable ways of pulling, and yet whose innocent, whose always ingenuous agitation of their members he has found means to make them think of themselves as delightfully free and easy" (p. 107). It is not hard to recognize here the novelist's policy of supervised freedom, as exemplified in the late fiction and formalized in the prefaces and, to borrow a phrase from the preface to *The Ambassadors*, the "dissimulated calculation" of the master spirits of management. The teller of tales, James declares in the same preface, is a "handler of puppets," and the formal enclosures of plot ("Strether [is] encaged and provided for as 'The Ambassadors' encages and provides") are everywhere "artfully dissimulated."[27] It is no accident that James, the Master, calls the hotel-spirit a "master indeed" (p. 107).

26. Donald L. Mull, *Henry James's "Sublime Economy": Money as Symbolic Center in the Fiction* (Middletown: Wesleyan University Press, 1973), 168.

27. Henry James, Preface to *The Ambassadors*, in *The Art of the Novel* (New York: Scribner's, 1934), 319, 311, 321, 323.

IV

I have been arguing that James's account of the hotel-world displays the panoptic and normalizing techniques that constitute the American scene and also the proximate relation between his own techniques of representation and the mechanisms of managerial power. Moreover, if James dissimulates the relation between art and power, this dissimulation itself appears as one of the ruses of power: it is through its dissembling art of power that the hotel-spirit discreetly manages its scheme of closure. James's text does not simply "reproduce" panoptic and normalizing practices; rather, the Jamesian text participates in, and indeed promotes, the practical and theoretical search for more comprehensive and more tactful strategies of regulation.

We might even say that James's criticism of the Victorian novelist's loose and baggy monsters, and formalizing of a poetics of narrative, achieves for the novel the very discipline of form that Wells proposes to regulate the confused and untidy expedients of Victorian society. But such a collaboration between literary and social forms does not merely "collapse" the difference between these terms. On the contrary, it is necessary to speak of a production and even management of this difference between the literary and the political and of the ways in which this difference might function within a larger system of regulation. Crucially, I suggest that if James defends against the entanglement between art and power by advertising an essential incompatibility between literary and political interests, this advertised incompatibility and difference between the literary and the political—this segregation of art and power—in fact defends the very power structures it seems to defend against. The paradoxical form this defense of difference takes is the story told in the "good prose text" (p. 276) of Philadelphia.

Lincoln Steffens, in *The Shame of the Cities* (1904), declared Philadelphia to be the city of "corruption and contentment." Philadelphia was at once the preeminently "aristocratic" and "social" American city and, paradoxically, the most thoroughly corrupt. The city, Steffens observed, gives one "a sense of more leisure and repose than any other community," but this repose coexists with and is indeed sponsored by the lawless economic and political machine of the city: if Philadelphians are "hopelessly ring-ruled, they are 'complacent.'"[28] It is this "good neighbouring" of Philadelphia's "confirmed and content" society and the corruption of its "Infernal Machine" that centers James's account of the Quaker city (pp. 277, 284). The city, James notes, presented itself as "two distinct things":

> a Society, from far back, the society I had divined, the most genial and delightful one could think of, and then, parallel to this, and not within it, nor quite altogether above it, but beside it and beneath it, behind it and before it, enclosing it as in a frame of fire in which it still had the secret of keeping cool, a proportionate City, the most incredible that ever was, organized all for plunder and rapine, the gross satisfaction of official appetite, organized for eternal iniquity and impunity. [p. 283]

James's representation of Philadelphia explores the "secret of keeping cool" within the encircling fires of political corruption, the "mystery of the terms of the bargain" (p. 284) made by the "perfect Philadelphians" (p. 282) to maintain the peaceful coexistence of these two parallel but ostensibly separate cities. And James's reading of the Philadelphia story also indirectly and evasively exposes the "communication" between these two "distinct" provinces—the social and cultural city and the corrupt city of power.

James begins his account of Philadelphia by remarking that for the critical analyst "the last thing decently permitted him is to recognize incoherence" (p. 273). Earlier in *The American Scene*, James had expressed his yearning for an American site possessed of "the luxury of some such close and sweet and *whole* national consciousness as that of the Switzer and the Scot" (p.

---

28. Lincoln Steffens, *The Shame of the Cities* (1904; reprint ed., New York: Hill and Wang, 1957), 135, 134.

86). Philadelphia apparently provides both this coherence and this organic and communal wholeness. The city is marked by an "ordered charm and perfect peace" (p. 277). Fixed, rounded, and complete, Philadelphia represents "in the composed sense, a society" (p. 278). Like the stable world of the hotel, Philadelphian society is a world in perfect "social equilibrium" (p. 280), an equilibrium that again has both a social and an aesthetic dimension. Homogeneous, ordered, and settled, Philadelphia is a "little masterpiece of the creative imagination" (pp. 282–283), and having accomplished this finality of composition, the city reposes in the "secret of serenity": "Her imagination was at peace" (pp. 277, 278).

The Quaker society is above all a centered society. Contained within the stable equilibrium of a "practically self-sufficing little world" (p. 286), Philadelphian society occupies a charmed and "closed circle that would find itself happy enough if only it could remain closed enough" (p. 286). This sense of encirclement and enclosure is enforced, in part, by the city's kinship structure, its "scheme of consanguinity" (p. 279). In the Quaker city of brothers and sisters, one discovers a "state of infinite cousinship" (p. 280) that guarantees the city's organic and intimate coherence. Moreover, the closed circle of Friends is reinforced by an insular vernacular, an exclusive idiom virtually "*constituting* the society that employed it" (p. 287). In all, Philadelphia's confined unity of composition expresses itself in a figure which, as we will see in a moment, serves as the rhetorical analogue for the city's circular scheme of life, the tautology: "Philadelphia was, yes, beyond cavil, solely and singly Philadelphian" (p. 281).

The Philadelphia social circle is "built round" Independence Hall, the site that provides the "central something, the social *point de repère*" about which the city's life "revolve[s]" (p. 290). Serving as the model for the city's continuity of generations and centripetal associations, Independence Hall is the "superior connection" for the "nice family" and the architectural model for the "serenity and symmetry" and the "noble congruity" of the Philadelphia mode of life: its "character . . . everywhere hangs together and keeps itself up" (p. 289–292). More significantly, Independence Hall functions as the center of the Philadelphia "scheme" in its declared independence from the vulgar traffic of wealth and industry, from the parallel city of plunder and iniquity that "frames" the "Happy Family." The Hall centrally represents an "emphasis of detachment from the vulgar brush of things" (p. 289).

This emphatic detachment secures the Philadelphia scheme. More generally, it allows the "sane Society and pestilent City in the United States [to] successfully cohabit, each keeping it up with so little fear or flutter from the other" (p. 283). And this detachment neatly coincides with James's own avowed aversion to and evasion of the "mere monstrosities" of "trade and traffic, of organisation, political, educational, economic" (p. 297). Indeed, James here again confesses that his own "attention happened to be, or rather was obliged to be, confined to one view of the agreement" (p. 284), to one view of that "bargain" or "exchange" made by Society with the Infernal City. Both the Philadelphians and their analyst adopt the terms of a sort of mutual nonintervention pact.

But there is a certain tension between statement and performance in James's account of Philadelphia. The assertion that the city was "two distinct things," for instance, is not entirely compatible with the description James gives of the relation between Philadelphia's "Quaker purity" and the machinations of the "nefarious City" (p. 285). Even as he reiterates this "purity," James traces the mixed character of the Quaker society. Thus, if purity is signified by the "original Quaker drab" (p. 284), this drab unaccountably shows a " 'worldly' overscoring" under the influence of which it "flushes . . . to the prettiest pink." Clearly, this "flush" betrays the shame of an entanglement with the facts of power. The "accommodating Friend" is seen to accommodate precisely his "compromise" (p. 285) with the criminal City. The "criminaloid" inmixing is subtle, and the line between criminal and good citizen difficult to draw, "so that we never quite know where the drab has ended and the colour of the world has begun" (p. 285). But if the Society "gracefully veils" its compromised character, the Philadelphia "secret of a *modus vivendi*" is the veiled fact of this compromise, the criminal continuity of these united states. Hence the Happy Family remains "indifferent" to the trade and traffic of the world even as it "carries on the family business of buying and selling" (p. 284).

The secret of America's serenity has less to do with a discernible difference and distinction between the Society and the City than with an *in*difference to the *non*distinction. Nor does James's view of this compromised and compromising mode of life reduce to a simple charge of hypocrisy. Rather, the conscious pretense of the Happy Family is precisely its "virtue," its "admirable" and "heroic" character (p. 284). It is the *fiction* of its detachment that the family promotes, the fiction of an unviolated and closed circle distinct from the nefarious world of power and gain. The precariousness of this fiction of autonomy affects James as the "thrilled sense of a society dancing, all consciously, on the thin crust of a volcano" (p. 285), and James insists on the "bravery" of the performance.

If the Philadelphia scheme is, from one point of view, simply a lie, it also resembles Maggie's sustained pretense in *The Golden Bowl* that the family is happy and safe even as she knows that this is a fiction. It might be said, as Leo Bersani has suggested, that James's endorsement of Maggie's policy of pretense is an indication of the novelist's faith in the "superior finality of art" and "affirms the triumph of fictional composition over a powerfully resistant reality."[29] Such a faith is perhaps implicit in James's thrilled appreciation of the Philadelphia scheme and of the manner in which the perfect Philadelphians "keep up" their composed little world. But the problem here is in locating what "resistant reality" this "fictional composition" is finally superior to. With an emphasis similar to Bersani's, John Carlos Rowe asserts that James's "activity" in *The American Scene* is one of "giving shape and dimension to the formless and often chaotic

---

29. Leo Bersani, *A Future for Astyanax* (Boston: Little, Brown, 1976), 146.

world he encounters." The Jamesian "values of formal composition" are set in opposition to a "formless" world.[30]

But the America that James encounters is anything but formless—"there are a thousand forms of this ubiquitous American force" (p. 106)—and it is a finality of composition that defines both the hotel-world and Philadelphia society. These rather automatic oppositions of "composition" and "reality" are instances of what has been called the "conservative fictionalist tradition" in Anglo-American criticism, a tradition that insists on a basic antinomy between the forms of fiction and a chaotic reality resistant to form.[31] But a compositional value characterizes the structures of power and the initiatives of James's art both. There is, to adapt the terms that the Philadelphia scheme provides, a *family resemblance* between the discourse of power and the discourse of art: it is just this resemblance that the Philadelphia scheme—and the critical schemes that reiterate its terms—rewrite as a radical opposition or difference.

Both the Philadelphian and the critical fiction are finally grounded by an ideological distinction between art and power, and James names the way in which this distinction is kept up, and the way it functions, in the closing pages of his treatment of the Quaker city. We might say that, like Strether in *The Ambassadors*, the Philadelphians and James himself have self-consciously tried to "suppose nothing." But one can hardly suppose nothing *as* a supposition, and if this self-contradiction defines the double discourse of James's art—the simultaneous recognition and disavowal of the criminal continuity between aesthetic and political practices—James here exposes this very duplicity. James confesses that the fiction that he has both represented and celebrated is the "art in particular of cultivating, with such gaiety as might be, a brave civic blindness" (p. 299). The fiction of the Philadelphia scheme—"the happy family given up, though quite on 'family' lines, to all the immediate beguilements and activities" (p. 299)—operates through a willed blindness to its entanglement with the family business and "crime" of power. The evasive art practiced by the analyst who has inscribed himself into this scheme similarly "works as a blind." James's policy of representation in *The American Scene* is, to borrow a phrase from his late story of New York, "Crapy Cornelia," a "policy of blindness."

From a somewhat different perspective, these blinds set up between the Happy Family and the criminal World, and between the domains of the fictional and the political, might be understood in terms of what Fredric Jameson has called ideological *"strategies of containment"*—intellectual or formal strategies that allow "what can be thought to seem internally coherent in its own terms, while repressing the unthinkable . . . which lies beyond its boundaries."[32] What the Philadelphia scheme makes unthinkable is the relation between the two segregated but nevertheless communicating and even cohabiting members of Philadelphia's extended family. If the domestic circle and frame of fire are insistently opposed in James's representation of Philadelphia, these demarcated and segregated domains are, at the same time, suspended in relation to each other, apparently at odds but in fact tautologically related. It is the story of this relation, and of the fiction of difference on which it depends, that the Philadelphia story ultimately tells.

James closes his account of the Quaker city by implicitly rereading the Philadelphia mode of enclosure, security, and confinement that he has traced. Or rather, one must call this closing not a rereading but simply *another* reading, not integrated or synthesized with his earlier account but instead set beside it, suspended in relation to it, and hence duplicating the system of containment and suspension that forms its subject. If the Happy Family represents one center of the Philadelphia scheme, there is another site that recapitulates the Philadelphian emphasis on

32. Fredric Jameson, *The Political Unconscious: Narrative as a Socially Symbolic Act* (Ithaca: Cornell University Press, 1981), 102, 183–84.

detachment and insularity, and the ideological blindness—or better, the ideology of blindness—on which it depends. The Pennsylvania Penitentiary provides an alternate point de repère for the Philadelphia way. The prison appears as the "one excrescence on the vast smooth surface" (p. 229), but it threatens finally to subsume the city itself. And the family and the prison ultimately appear as the twin sites of a single, albeit split and conflicting, scheme of regulation, a scheme that relies centrally on strategies of containment and differentiation, on what we might call a regulative deployment of difference.

The prison is surrounded by "defensive moats" that mark its separation from the city, and this system of separation is repeated within the structure itself. The Pennsylvania prison, as James notes, was the "first flourishing example of the strictly cellular system, the complete sequestration of the individual prisoner" (p. 299). This comprehensive scheme of confinement is again imaged in the form of a tautology: "A prison has, at the worst, the massive majesty, the sinister peace, of a prison." One begins to detect, however, a compelling resemblance between the tautological peace of the prison and the serenity and security of the city's closed circle, and the pressure of this resemblance immediately asserts itself: "But," the passage continues, "this huge house of sorrow affected me as, uncannily, of the City itself, the City of all the cynicisms and impunities against which my friends had, from far back, kept plating, as with the old silver of their sideboards, the armour of their social consciousness" (p. 300). The passage enacts a bizarre fantasmatics of confinement. The defensive line between the prison and the criminal City is explicitly breached, but a second cordon sanitaire becomes visible. If the Quaker Friends have attempted to defend themselves from a criminal continuity with the nefarious City, the defense is accomplished through another movement of confinement: a confinement within a "silver-plated" and sequestered social consciousness that erects an ideological armor of difference and detachment.

A series of uncanny relations are thus suggested, relations not merely between the plundering Infernal City and the house of crime but also between the enclosed space of the perfectly composed Society and the quarantined order of the disciplinary fortress, between, finally, the Protestant business of purity and what Weber described as tbe "iron cage" of capitalist organization.[33] As James would have known from his readings of Dickens's *American Notes* (which he here cites [p. 300]), the Pennsylvania Penitentiary was erected and organized under the direct influence of the Quakers, whose contribution was the plan of complete sequestration. The plan was based on an analogy between the monastic, penitential cell and the prison cell; as James remarks, the penitentiary possessed "almost the harmony of the convent"; it was a carceral from which "the worst of the rigour has visibly been drawn" (p. 301, 300). The Quaker reformatory was, as Foucault has shown, perhaps the most influential model of the "gentle way of punishment." Combining a monastic confinement with an applied principle of disciplined work, the Philadelphia plan linked the economy of discipline with the discipline of capitalist economy: the prison cell becomes "in this protestant society the instrument by which one may reconstitute both *homo oeconomicus* and the religious conscience."[34]

The Pennsylvania principle of separation, Michael Ignatieff argues, depended on a system of linkages, on "hidden affinities between Quaker piety and Enlightenment materialism" that inured the inmate to industry and to discipline alike. The new prisons also, Ignatieff adds, "played a role in the enforcement of family discipline."[35] In the previous chapter, I have indicated the ways in which the family was invested with techniques of policing and normalization. We detect as well a hidden affinity between the institution of the family and the practice of the total institution. If, as David Rothman suggests, "the family was the

33. Max Weber, *The Protestant Ethic and the Spirit of Capitalism*, trans. T. Parsons (New York: Scribner's, 1958), 181.

34. Foucault, *Discipline and Punish*, 123.

35. Michael Ignatieff, *A Just Measure of Pain: The Penitentiary in the Industrial Revolution, 1750–1850* (New York: Pantheon, 1978), 109.

model of institutional organization," these institutions were explicitly designed to supplement and support (breakdowns in) the practice of the family; the total institution becomes at the same time the model of the family. Hence its "tactic was to advise the family to fulfill its tasks well. By giving advice and demonstrating the awful consequences of an absence of discipline, critics would inspire the family to a better performance."[36] A circular movement is established between the registers of the family and the disciplinary institution, and the differences between these two "opposed" registers are retained in a strategy of mutual reinforcement. In brief, the "detachment" of the family from the nefarious world is protected as long as the family disciplines itself; the larger institutions of discipline are always in place to support the family should it fail to maintain its "autonomy." An economical principle of "conversion" is established between conflicting and opposed domains.

There is more to say about this circular system by which the separation between public and private domains is "managed" within a larger alignment and alliance of disciplinary forces.[37] For now it may be noted that the Philadelphia strategy of containment suppresses just this circular or tautological relation between the enclosure of the family and the enclosure of the prison. The Quaker fiction of difference disclaims the links between the family and the world and, by extension, between the house of fiction and the prison house. But James, inspecting the penitentiary, finds it difficult to define the difference between the convicts and the pure citizens of the city, between the confinement of the city and the multiple confinements of the Quaker scheme. The prisoners represent "cases of the vocation." Commenting on the "refinement" wrought in a reprieved murderer "lounging and chatting" in a "sunny Club"—a club not unlike the country clubs that James sees as the American family institution *par excellence*—James cannot discover the distinguishing in-

36. David J. Rothman, *The Discovery of the Asylum: Social Order and Disorder in the New Republic* (Boston: Little, Brown, 1971), 234, 71.
37. I will be addressing this topic at greater length in my final chapter.

signia of criminality: "Was the fact of prison *all* the mere fact of opportunity, and the fact of freedom all the mere fact of the absence of it?" (p. 301). Opportunity as confinement, freedom as the absence of opportunity: the prison is only the most visible site of a general imprisonment within a criminaloid and disciplinary society.

"The suggestions here," James remarks, "were vast," but the novelist closes by self-consciously setting them aside. He confesses that his "imagination must defend itself as it can," and the defense takes the form of a resort to a transparently "prompt conclusion," a final strategy of containment that "kept, in a manner, the excrescence, as I have called it, on the general scene, within bounds" (pp. 300–301). The foregrounded qualifiers, however, self-consciously give the scheme away; the excrescence has already exceeded its bounds. James thus reassumes the Philadelphian "social character and its practical philosophy" (p. 301) of a brave blindness in order to "clear" the general scene. He retreats to an old country house "virtually distant from town" and, "with his back to the fire," celebrates the virtuous "freedom of movement" afforded by this romantic reserve of the "'old order'" (p. 302). But the country house is "virtually" and not actually distant from the machinations of the City, and standing with his back to the fire, James also represents his turning of the back to the nefarious "frame of fire" that is the Infernal City. Through a series of devious detours and indirections, the secret of the Philadelphia compromise is reenacted and reenacted as the secret of the Jamesian fiction.

V

What the "text" of Philadelphia reveals then is a surreptitious linkage of aesthetic and political practices, a linkage secured through the fiction of the mutual exclusion or even autonomy of these domains. Perhaps James's most elaborate treatment of the link between artistic and political practices occurs, appropriately enough, in his account of the political center of America's great representative democracy, Washington, D.C. Washington is both the political and administrative capital and the " 'artistic' Federal City" (p. 356); it is both the city of power and the "City of Conversation" (p. 342). James's representation of Washington becomes not merely an investigation of political policies of representation but also, more generally, an exposure of what we have called a politics of representation. The account of Washington focuses the relation between James's art of representation and the art of power and makes even more explicit the relation with which we have been implicitly concerned from the start—the alliance between discourse and power, between the question of our speech and the subject of power.

Washington clearly restates the equation between art and blindness that we have been tracing. James begins his reading of the artistic capital by celebrating the effect of the Washington spring—"the great artist of the season" (p. 332). The natural artist "dress[es] up" the city and prepares it "for social, for human intercourse, making it in fine publicly presentable, with an energy of renewal and an effect of redemption not often to be noted, I imagine, on other continents" (p. 332). But this "effect" is immediately revealed as a process of dissimulation and even deception. The spring is a "voluminous veil," and it veils the area of social intercourse that James purportedly evades—the "hard little facts" (p. 336) of political and economic life that Washington administers. The art that James initially celebrates is an art of omission and suppression. It refuses to touch the social surface until that surface has been "swept clean" of the facts of life: "The business is clearly to get rid of them as far as may be, to cover and smother them; dissimulating with the biggest, freest brush their impertinence and their ugliness" (p. 333). The "masking, dissimulating" season evokes an image of redemption only by "screen[ing]" the "as yet unsurmounted bourgeois character of the whole," and produces its charming effects by engaging a policy of blindness: Washington is "charming in proportion as you don't see it" (p. 335).

Once again incorporating himself into the scheme that he is representing, James aligns his strategies of representation with the practices of Washington's diplomatic community. If the diplomats substitute for a harder currency the "medium of exchange" of "smiles and inflections," if they are "pledged alike to penetration and to discretion," James expresses a willingness to adopt at least provisionally this diplomatic pretense, this double gesture of penetration and discreet dissimulation. He can, like the ambassadors, tactfully screen his "'real' sentiments" (p. 334) and "diplomatically, patriotically pretend . . . that such a Washington *was* the 'real' one" (p. 335). The way in which an art of illusion displaces what James agrees to call the "*real* Washington" could not be more clearly marked.

But James's equation of his art of representation with the techniques of diplomacy is not entirely on all fours with such a radical antinomy between the "illusory" and the "real." The ambassadors are of course representatives and "delegates of Powers" (p. 334), and their mode of representation is a mode of political action. Theirs is literally an art *of* power, and their ostensible blindness to the operations of power conceals a strategic collaboration between a masking, screening art and the techniques of power. James's account of Washington evasively and diplomatically discloses such a collaboration.

Washington, like Philadelphia, is a two-sided city. The capital presents "two distinct faces." Relegated to the "back of the scene," there is the public, official, imperial city; in the "foreground," however, was a "different thing, a thing that, ever so quaintly, seemed to represent the force really in possession"— the social city or "City of Conversation." Although this foreground consists but "of a small company of people engaged perpetually in conversation," the city of conversation effectively displaces the city of power: "This little society easily became . . . the city itself, *the* national capital and the greater part of the story" (p. 340).

Perhaps most evident here is the absolute break between these two scenes and the self-conscious *nonreferentiality* of the city of conversation: "The charming company of the fore-

ground . . . referred itself so little to the sketchy back-scene."
Talking past the discourses of business and power, the social city
cultivates a certain "ignorance" and expresses an "organized
indifference to the vulgar vociferous Market" (p. 342). The role
of the city of conversation is apparently "to make one forget," at
least for the moment, those subjects represented by the city of
power, and the conversation of the social city seems essentially,
as Wells ironically observed, an affair of negation and omission.
Washington paradoxically "knew nothing of the great American
interest"; there are, as James later remarks about Richmond,
"no *references*" (p. 371).

But the "story" told by the city of conversation thus becomes
rather difficult to locate. We must predicate, of course, a "general subject of all the conversation" (p. 342), but if the social city
knows nothing, refers to nothing, what does it talk about? The
answer that James proposes returns us to the figure that domi-
nates *The American Scene,* the tautology: "Washington talks about
herself, and about almost nothing else" (pp. 342–343). Insistently self-referential, the subject of Washington conversation is
its pursuit of itself as a possible topic of discourse. Washington's
speech is an attempt to "talk itself . . . into a *subject* for conversation." Not surprisingly, the city of conversation evokes for James
another image of confinement, the image of "some big buzzing
insect which keeps bumping against a treacherous mirror" (p.
343).

This specular confinement is the "embarrassment" of the city
of conversation. Clearly, it is also the embarrassment that has
traditionally been taken to define James's own fictional practice.
In its elliptical representation of its "subject," in its conversion of
matters of reference into strategies of self-reference, in the circular unity by which the events of the novel mirror his own
compositional initiatives, the Jamesian fiction is, like the city of
conversation, a "treacherous mirror." But the social city also
reproduces the counterside of this embarrassment. If the triumph (or defect) of James's fiction is the tautological coherence
produced by the perfect fit between his processes of composition

(his method) and his novelistic "worlds" (their fate), this is also the generative principle of that fiction. Thus, even as he traces the negating movements of the social city's talk, James asserts its constitutive power: the city of conversation offers, above all, a "fresh experiment of constitutive, creative talk" (p. 344). Talking, it has been suggested, is not merely the register of events in the Jamesian text. Speech—"really constructive dialogue, dialogue organic and dramatic, speaking for itself, representing and embodying substance and form"—promotes and produces events.[38] The "history of the voice," James observes in the lecture delivered during his American tour, "The Question of Our Speech," is the "history of the people": "our social relations" are "verily constituted" by our speech.[39] Washington conversation, ironically self-conscious and self-referential as it is, invokes for the novelist of conversation the possibility of a new social order, the possible evolution of a "new kind of civic consciousness." The attempt of the social city to talk itself into a subject represents, from this point of view, the attempt to talk into existence, to constitute and to compose a fresh vision of America. The initial elision of references and "general elimination" effected by the city of conversation might be read as a preparatory clearing of the scene, a provisional erasure of the sordid facts that opens a space for the inscription of a revised and renewed America. If social relations are constituted by our speech, then the project of this really constructive dialogue is the realization "for public uses . . . of the whole aesthetic law" (p. 357).

This aesthetic ambition Laurence Holland has identified as the Jamesian "determination to forge or shape a changing world, to create a society, to take his place in a community-in-the-making by joining in the process of making it."[40] More recently, Holland has emphasized the "energy of renewal" and "effect of redemption" inherent in James's representation of

---

38. James, Preface to *The Awkward Age*, in *The Art of the Novel*, 106.
39. James, *The Question of Our Speech*, 34.
40. Holland, *The Expense of Vision*, ix.

Washington, a representation that is not simply a "repetition" but rather an invocation of social possibilities.[41] We have seen that this renewal and redemption are presented as merely "illusory." But extending the terms of Holland's argument, it might be said that the apparent trivializing of the aesthetic involved in this contraposition of the illusory and the "real" in fact protects and affirms that aesthetic: indeed, the artistic representation could only serve as a model for renewal *if* it diverged from the real.

I have been questioning, however, just this radical distinction between the aesthetic and the actual. Clearly, the city of conversation reinvents the terms of the Jamesian aesthetic and social project. But implicit in this model of a redemptive aesthetic is the notion of the discursive, and more particularly, of "the literary," as essentially autonomous, as standing free from the constraints of the real. The Jamesian novel has been appropriated to support such an aesthetic of autonomy. The "organic" adjustments of content to form or of subject to treatment in James's novels have evoked, in Jamesian criticism, an inward commentary on the tautological and intransitive character of the Jamesian text. The tautological coherence of form and content in the Jamesian text has been taken to define the intrinsic literariness of the novel; the collateral "intransitivity" of literary discourse has become the measure of the intrinsic difference between literary and political practices. It would be possible to trace the history of this difference, the progressive demarcation, segregation, and splitting of literary and other discursive practices during the course of the nineteenth century, and I shall return to this topic in the next chapter. For the moment we may note that cultural historians such as Raymond Williams have indicated the process by which "literature" was defined against other discourses, specialized and professionalized, in the nineteenth century.[42] In *The Order of Things*, Foucault suggests that "the isola-

---

41. Holland, "Representation and Renewal," 414.

tion of a particular language whose mode of being is 'literary' "
takes place in the the last century, during which literature became "progressively more differentiated" from rival discourses
and enclosed "within a radical intransitivity," detached from and
opposed to all other forms of discourse.[43]

By this route, the literary has come to represent the "outside" of power. What I have been emphasizing here is the way
in which this externality of the literary to the political functions, the ways in which the "oppositional" character of literary
discourse may function within a larger field of discursive and
political practices. If, for instance, the organic adjudication of
the imperatives of form and content in the Jamesian text have
been taken to define the self-referential literariness of the
novel, we have seen that, on the contrary, the Jamesian principle of organicism registers the immanence of power in the
novel and ultimately appears as an aesthetic duplication and
formalizing of social practices of normalization. On another
level, if the redemptive aesthetic that James invokes in *The
American Scene* depends upon a romantic departure from the
real, we have seen that Wells's equation of the technological
and the artistic, for example, poses a fundamentally different
model for the recreation of America, a model that also "fic-
tively" departs from the real and equally relies upon the creative and constitutive power of discourse. Yet if one reads here
not an intrinsic difference between literary and political practices but instead a certain alignment and alliance of tactics and
interests, one should not simply "write off" the difference between literary and political domains, but rather indicate the

42. Raymond Williams, *Marxism and Literature* (Oxford: Oxford University
Press, 1977), 45–54. See also John Gross, *The Rise and Fall of the Man of Letters*
(New York: Macmillan, 1969); William Charvat, *The Profession of Authorship in
America, 1800–1870*, ed. Matthew J. Bruccoli (Columbus: Ohio State University
Press, 1968).

43. Michel Foucault, *The Order of Things: An Archaeology of the Human Sciences*
(New York: Vintage, 1973), 300.

ways in which this difference itself may be made to work within a larger network of power-discourse relations. The very notion of the externality of literary to political practices may support the very structures of power that the literary has been seen to resist; the notion of an intrinsic and subversive literary difference may provide the illusory outside and alternative to power that makes that power tolerable.

I am not suggesting that the literary always and in principle is on the side of power, though I have been insisting that the double discourse of the later nineteenth-century novel indeed provides an almost programmatic model of disciplinary and normalizing practices. I *am* suggesting that the notion that the literary always and in principle stands apart from and subverts structures of power may function ideologically to support the very power it seems to resist. For one thing, as we will see in a moment, the almost automatic opposition of a creative aesthetics to a constraining politics precisely covers the "productiveness" of modern apparatuses of power. For another, the notion of an autonomous (literary) discourse effectively screens the filiations between power and discourse in modern society. If James's treatment of Washington, for instance, holds out for an intrinsic difference between an aesthetic and creative power of speech and the hard facts of power, the chapter on Washington closes by implicitly posing an alternate reading of the relations between power and discourse. The city of conversation is finally, in fact, reinscribed within the city of power, and the creative power of speech that James has celebrated appears not merely as a "tribute to the aesthetic law" (p. 361) but instead, or rather at the same time, as the mode of imposition of a somewhat different kind of law.

James throughout represents the capital as a field of representations. Not only the city of conversation but also the city of power is explicitly a verbal space. James speaks of the "great general text" of the capital, of the "exclusively political page" of the federal city, of the "loud monosyllable . . . uttered" by the Washington monument (pp. 353, 352, 355). Indeed, the question of what "the Washington to come [will] have to 'say'" (p. 358) is addressed at once to the city of conversation and to the city of power. Above all, the Capitol is a "vast and many-voiced creation," one of the great "homes of debate" (p. 359), and this voice is literally the voice of power: the Capitol literally speaks into existence America's future, imposing its representations and law on the continent. If initially, as I have noted, James presents the city of conversation as the "real" locus of power in the capital—it "seemed to represent the force really in possession" (p. 340)—it is finally the status of this representation that he discloses. Nor is this verbal representation of power revealed as simply an illusion. James finally foregrounds precisely a power of representation—the discursive practices of the state— and these practices comprehensively reiterate his own.

Significantly, James closes his account of the federal city by searching for just those subjects that he began by getting rid of— the "hard facts" of power and history. Entering the White House, James invokes the ghosts of the past, the violence and bloody sacrifice that have made the state potent. The White House is "haunted ground," but James finds it hard to "'place' the strange, incongruous blood-drops . . . on that revised and freshened page" (p. 355). The revisions to which James refers are the recent restorations of the executive mansion, but the passage invites us to read this process of textual revision as an elision of the blood of America's past itself, as a part of what James later calls the "eternal bowdlerization" (p. 374) of history that defines the American scene. If earlier a process of elision, or censorship, appeared as the preparatory cleansing for the social city's experiment in fresh, creative talk, it now appears that the city of power works a remarkably similar technique of omission and suppression. It is by erasing the traces of power that power "represents" itself: "The wide-spread wings of the general Government . . . affect us, in the prospect, as great fans that, by their mere tremor, will blow the work, at all steps and stages, clean and clear, disinfect it quite ideally of any germ of the job" (p. 356).

James's diplomatic posture toward the capital, his cultivated discretion and blindness to the subject of power, collate perfectly with the strategic disavowal of power enforced by the institutions of the state. Washington "rakes the prospect, it rakes the continent," but the violence of power is artfully screened: the "centre" of power presents only its immaculate "marble fronts" and "vague bright forms" (p. 363). At the close of his account of Washington, James, the dispossessed analyst, discovers a curious counterpart in a "trio of Indian braves, braves dispossessed of forest and prairie," and their presence on the steps of the Capitol focuses his vision of the violent usurpations that have constituted the present state. They present "an image in itself immense, but foreshortened and simplified—reducing to a single smooth stride the bloody footsteps of time" (p. 364). But here again, power has covered its tracks, and James cannot find a reference to the violence of history in the revised text of the state. The passage ends with a double vision of history that registers also the double discourse of power, a discourse that at once effects its violence and erases the traces of that violence: "One rubbed one's eyes, but there, at its highest polish, shining in the beautiful day, was the brazen face of history, and there, all about one, immaculate, the printless pavements of the State" (p. 364).

The supple mechanisms of power deploy tactics of evasion and censorship that, we have seen, characterize both the city of conversation and James's own strategies of representation. In a sense, the "two distinct faces" of the capital are in fact two faces of the same coin. Moreover, James's account of Washington suggests not merely a point of intersection between literary and political discursive practices but also that the very policies of representation that seem most comprehensively to resist power prove to be perhaps the very means of securing the success of that power. Power is tolerable only if it masks a part of itself, but this is not to say that power simply operates "behind" or "below" its representations. This account suggests that these representations are not merely screens or "illusions" but also modes of exercising power. If James, as we have seen, tries to protect the aesthetic by displacing the reality of power with an artful illusion, this artful evasion of the actual is also an art of power. And is it not possible to say that the critical practices that shuffle away the links between the aesthetic and the political are part of the same ideology of power? Above all, James's account suggests that the discourse of power is not a monologue but rather a dispersed and differentiated, even contradictory, network of voices. Modern social practices of regulation operate by way of, and not in spite of, different and contradictory representations; they display a "splitting" of power but also a power of splitting— display irreducible conflicts but also a comprehensive investment in techniques of conflict management.

VI

It might be objected, however, that in tracing the multiple entanglements between James's techniques of representation and the tactics of power, I have ignored just those strata of James's text that have made possible my own reading. The policies of blindness and containment that form the "program" of *The American Scene* reveal their covert complicity with the social technologies of power that James claims to disown. But these claims, I have argued, are perhaps too insistently foregrounded. James perhaps too transparently gives himself away in constant moves of self-subversion and self-ironization. There is nothing more evident about *The American Scene* than its improvisatory byplay, its rapid movement of voices and slipperiness of perspectives, its ironic exposure of its own procedures. The "mode" of James's discourse—the style of deviation and excess—can be seen to subvert both his own formalizing initiatives and the concentric organizations of power. Acknowledging that he is always trapped within the confines of power, James attempts to devise strategies of resistance, and his tactics of resistance everywhere interrupt and defer closure even as the novelist's search for form inevitably aspires to it. The very contradictions and incoherences of the text display such resistance. Thus, even as he values the "finer feeling for the enclosure," even as he seeks settled forms in which beauty can "splendidly rest," the "restless" analyst's speech, it might be argued, slips through the gaps of power: his discourse proceeds from "between the . . . interstices of the enclosures" (p. 448). If the caged worlds of hotel-civilization allow "scant occasion for the wandering apart which always forms, under the law of the herd, the intenser joy," James everywhere violates this law through the "sweet subterfuge" and eccentricity of his wandering and "straying" discourse (449–451).

There is no question about James's investment in these strategies of resistance. Nor is it difficult to locate more precisely the form this resistance takes. Escaping from the closed order of the Waldorf-Astoria, for instance, James recounts an extraordinary incident. He escapes, he says, "to walk the streets," on a "pursuit" that "irresistibly solicited . . . the observer" (p. 107). This pursuit involves "an adventure, I admit, as with some strident, battered, questionable beauty, truly some 'bold bad' charmer" (p. 108). The hotel-world, we have seen, through its consummate system of management, imposes a "rigour with which any appearance of pursued or desired adventure is kept down." The "promiscuous passage" (p. 108) that follows on his confinement within this scene of repression registers the liberated observer's reaction to the enforced conformity of the hotel-world. And if it is hard to see James in the role of a walker of the streets in pursuit of a street walker, what this passage records is the "state of desire" that James explicitly opposes to the constricting organizations of power.

This state of desire can scarcely be located in the democratic consistency of the United States. The American scene imposes a "blank conformity to convention" and reduces all to the "common mean" and the "decent average" (pp. 198, 442). Like the federal city, America is a disinfected landscape, cleaned and cleared of excess and deviation, and the remarkable health of the social body represents the achievement of a "general *sterilized* state" (p. 414). The immanent rule of the norm compels conformity, and crucially, within this normative scenario, desire can only be regarded as a deviation into abnormality, indeed, as *vice*. But in America "the implication of vices . . . is as absent for evil as for good" and not merely absent but virtually inconceivable: the "American town-appearance . . . amounts, everywhere, to something intenser than the implied absence of 'vice'; it amounts to a sort of registered absence of the conception or the imagination of it" (pp. 45, 311).

It is the pathology of desire that James pursues. Reading the American scene in the "light of literary desire" (p. 69), James searches for the "smutch of imputation" (p. 47) that would constitute at least the "show" of life. For the story seeker, it is the infraction or deviation that makes a story. In his preface to *The Spoils of Poynton*, for instance, James speaks of the "germ" of his story, and this germ is both the seed from which the tale "organically" grows and a sort of infection. The "wandering word" that James overhears "communicates the virus of suggestion," and the initial implication of a subject for treatment operates as a "prick of inoculation; the *whole* of the virus . . . being infused by that single touch."[44] Deviation from the normal state constitutes narrative for James, and, I am suggesting, it is the vice or disease of desire that James opposes to the regulative schemes of the managerial society.

In *The American Scene* this vice appears perhaps most clearly in James's excessive economy of representation. Although at times James insists on a balance and equilibrium of "reading in" and "reading out" in his account of America, more often he discards this "superstition" of reciprocity (p. 273). Breaking with the law of the equilibrium, it becomes a "question—as I have indeed already sufficiently shown—of what one read *into* anything, not of what one read out of it" (p. 68). For the interpreter America is a "pale page into which he might read what he liked" (p. 384), and this liberty of interpretation is, James confesses, a deviation into vice, "the vice of reading too much meaning into simple intentions" (p. 328).

The name that James gives to these liberating representa-

---

44. James, Preface to *The Spoils of Poynton*, in *The Art of the Novel*, 119, 121.

tional excesses is of course the romance. The Jamesian romance is the "subterfuge of our thought and our desire" that extravagantly evades and exceeds the actual, and *The American Scene* can in many ways be read as a detour into romance.[45] Recounting his rail journey through Georgia, for instance, James speaks of "squeezing a sense" from his uniform material, of "reading heaven knows what instalment of romance into a mere railroad matter" (p. 429). The novelist everywhere acknowleges a willingness "to strain a point . . . for the romance" (p. 36). Nor does the recourse to romance indicate merely a desire to escape the real. In the manner I earlier suggested, the romantic exceeding of the real is part of what James calls in his preface to "The Lesson of the Master" the "high and helpful public, and, as it were, civic use of the imagination." Responding to the rebuke that he has in his tales been "citing celebrities without analogues and painting portraits without models," James defends his literary license by appealing to a use of the imagination that self-consciously outstrips the actual. His art, James declares, is an attempt to project the ideal alternative and "antidote" to a limited and limiting social scene: "When it's not a campaign, of a sort, on behalf of the something better (better than the obnoxious, the provoking object) that blessedly, as is assumed, *might* be, it's not worth speaking of."[46] This is the sort of campaign that *The American Scene* implicitly invokes.

I have been suggesting that James's artful evasion of the actual can be read as a strategy of resistance, that James's excessive representational "vices," his invocation of the liberating provocations of the romance, operate to resist an encaging reality at the same time that they express the desire, simply enough, for "something better." There is certainly nothing unusual about such an opposition between the resistances of desire and re-

45. The quoted phrase is from James's Preface to *The American*, in *The Art of the Novel*, p. 32. On the Jamesian romance, see, for instance: Laurence Holland, *The Expense of Vision*, 64–66; Holland's more recent "Representation and Renewal" emphasizes the romance imperatives in *The American Scene*.

46. James, Preface to "The Lesson of the Master," in *The Art of the Novel*, 222.

pressive social strategies of equilibration and immobilization. In-deed, the "literary" in at least one school of recent critical prac-tice is precisely the discourse of desire. "History is what hurts," Fredric Jameson, for example, has written: "It is what refuses desire and sets inexorable limits to individual as well as collective praxis. . . . The Real is thus—virtually by definition in the fallen world of capitalism—that which resists desire."[47] Literature, it is argued, tells the story of this resistant desire, and thus, virtually by definition, literature resists the real, the historical.

But I have been questioning just this opposing of art and power, this tendency even on the part of the most politically conscious critics to depoliticize and to dehistoricize the literary text. More specifically, in my account of *The Golden Bowl* I have tried to show that desire is not in fact subversive of the "world of capitalism" but is instead constitutive of its power; the novel displays a radical entanglement between the movements of de-sire and the moves of power. It might be said that the very notion of power as having only an external hold on a resistant desire is perhaps the most effective means by which capitalist power is made tolerable. As Foucault observes, "power as a pure limit set on freedom is, at least in our society, the general form of its acceptability."[48]

Put somewhat differently, if power is pure limit, desire—and the literary discourse of desire—is a haven or escape from power; if power is merely repressive, desire (the literary) may slip, as it were, through the interstices of power. But we have seen that James's later work traces the "positive" and not merely the repressive character of power relations. Furthermore, far from escaping from the mechanisms of power, James's tech-niques of representation discreetly reproduce social modes of policing and regulation and reproduce them the more power-fully in their very discretion, in the very gesture of disowning the shame of power. I want to close this account by clarifying the

---

47. Fredric Jameson, *The Political Unconscious*, 102, 183–84.
48. Michel Foucault, *The History of Sexuality*, trans. Robert Hurley (New York: Pantheon, 1978), 86.

nexus of power and desire in *The American Scene* and the art of power that it secures.

Social programs of normalization, we have seen, not merely tolerate but require resistances; the exception constitutes the rule. James explicitly contraposes the moves of desire and the excesses of romance to social movements of normalization; the "virus" of narrative is a pathological deviation from the norm. But if James equates story with the vice of deviation, the mechanism he invokes, it will be recalled, is that of "inoculation," perhaps the exemplary type of the normalizing procedure: disease is introduced into the organism in order to promote a resistance to disease, in order to resecure health and normality. It is this circular operation—this normalizing detour into abnormality—that defines what I have called the double discourse of the late nineteenth-century novel in general and the Jamesian text in particular. The ostensible pathology and criminality of the realist text, for instance, cover for a covert policing action.

The realist novel represents and embraces vice, criminality, and deviation, and the romantic deviations from "the real" in this fiction constitute an aesthetics of pathology. The events in what Frank Norris, for example, calls "romantic fiction" must be "twisted from the ordinary," must depart from the "commonplace" into the "extraordinary, the vast, the monstrous." The naturalistic or "romantic realism" practiced by Zola "is the kind of fiction that takes cognizance of variations from the type of normal life."[49] But this romantic deviation from the normal type operates as a form of inoculation; the introduction of pathology and disequilibrium opens a space for normalizing moves to operate. Again, Zola provides perhaps the clearest account of the paradoxical economy by which the irregularities of the realist text reconstitute social techniques of regulation and equilibration.

For Zola as for James, pathology and disequilibrium make

---

49. Frank Norris, "Zola as a Romantic Writer" and "A Plea for Romantic Fiction," in *McTeague* (New York: Norton, 1977), 309, 310, 314.

story. The reason "why Balzac has insisted so much on Baron Hulot, has analyzed him with such scrupulous care," Zola argues in his discussion of *La Cousine Bette,* is that Hulot represents a "grave infection that poisons society." Hulot's excessive desires break the "social circle." But the novelist's scrupulous insistence on infection is a vigilance of care that ultimately masters the deviant and excessive: "The experiment bears upon [Hulot] above all because it was a question of mastering the phenomenon of this passion in order to direct it; admit that it is possible to cure Hulot, or at least hold him in and make him inoffensive, at once the drama has no more raison d'être, equilibrium has been re-established, or, better, the health of the social body."[50] Desire and disequilibrium are at once the raison d'être of narrative and the occasion for mastery to be exercised. The vice of desire is at once solicited and confiscated, and this suggests not an opposition between power and desire but rather that the production of desire cannot be separated from the production of power.

I am suggesting that the excesses of romance and desire that James sets against the structures of hotel-civilization are in fact crucial to the operation of these structures. The motto for the excessive policies of representation that we have identified in *The American Scene* might well be taken from the "homely moral" that James draws from his concluding discussion of the hotel-world of Saint Augustine: "When you haven't what you like you must perforce like, and above all misrepresent, what you have" (p. 457). Clearly, it is such a practice of (mis)representation that allows James to screen the truth and the facts of life that he wants to evade, to substitute a romantic pretense for a vulgar actuality. The problem, however, is that this passage refers not to his own aesthetic policies but instead to the artistic "hankey

---

50. Emile Zola, "The Experimental Novel," in *Documents of Modern Literary Realism,* ed. George J. Becker (Princeton: Princeton University Press, 1963), 179. The notion of deviation and disequilibrium as a narrative requirement has of course become a commonplace in structuralist poetics; I am attempting to suggest here what might be called a theoretical rewriting of this tactic of regulation and normalization.

pankey" and "faking" promoted by the master spirits of the
hotel-world. If Saint Augustine is the consummate hotel-world,
it is also a "mine of romance," meeting the "aesthetic need" of
the country through a process of representation and an "artistic
activity" that can scarcely be distinguished from James's own (p.
457).

James's account of the caged world of hotel-civilization emphasizes the panoptic and managerial supervision exercised by
the hotel-spirit, and we have already seen that the compositional
powers of the managerial spirit incite James's envy, reproduce
his own narrative panopticism. His account also reveals an apparently opposed but ultimately parallel side of the hotel's economy of organization. If the hotel-world contains desire, it at the
same time works to incite and even cultivate ideals and desires
that, in a circular fashion, it is organized to gratify. The hotel is
in fact a *machine of desire,* and its "mission" involves not only
"meeting all American ideals, but of creating . . . new and superior ones"; "its basis, in those high developments, is not that it
merely gratifies them as soon as they peep out, but that it lies in
wait for them, anticipates and plucks them forth even before
they dawn, setting them up almost prematurely and turning
their face in the right direction" (p. 440). With an insidious
expertise, the hotel-world creates and contains desire in a single
gesture. Promoting "extraordinary appetites" that can only be
"expensively sated," deferring that satisfaction by midwiving
and creating new and better ideals of fulfillment and self-real-
ization, the paradoxical economy of the hotel-world is not opposed to but empowered by a "pathos of desire" (pp. 440, 446).

Hotel-civilization deploys what might be called a *discipline of
desire.*[51] At one extreme, James finds his formalizing initiatives

---

51. In a provocative discussion of the links between capitalism and desire in
realist fiction, "*Sister Carrie's* Popular Economy," *Critical Inquiry* 7:2 (1980), 373–
90, Walter Benn Michaels argues that the realist novel and capitalism both rely
on an economy of desire and "powerful excess." Although I am indebted here to
Michaels's account, my own view is closer to that expressed in Foucault's *History
of Sexuality.* According to this view, the capitalist economy operates by setting up

comprehensively and ideally actualized in the achieved closure of the hotel-world; at the other, his attempts to exceed the actual in the direction of something better dramatically reinvented in the calculated excitation of appetite and excess by the romance world of the hotel. The hotel-spirit, which is for James the American spirit, elaborately recreates the "convention of the romance" (p. 457) and enlists the nation's artistic energies to supply "an inordinate *desire for taste*" (p. 446). The arts of the magazine illustrator, the draftsman, the journalist, the novelist, the dramatist, the genealogist, and the historian "are pressed . . . into the service" of the nation's "universal organizing passion" (pp. 458, 445). If James sees these arts as "clever fakes" presenting "subjects and situations" that do not in fact exist (p. 458), these counterfeits nevertheless invoke the same aesthetic and "patriotic yearning," the same desire for something better that backs James's own misrepresentations, his extemporizing of "portaits without models," his improvisatory "improvements" on the actual. Substituting for that which "is" the new and improved "might be," the technology of the hotel-world is the technology of romance.

This social technology of romance is perhaps most clearly expressed in the new genre that emerges to promote it. James calls the literary desire for a better world the romance. Hotel-civilization renames it the art of advertisement. The arts that James inventories are, of course, "forms of advertisement" (p. 443), the genre of the "money passion," the capitalist art par excellence. The emergence of the modern discourse of advertising at the turn of the century involved the "propagation of an aesthetic of mass industrialism,"[52] the creation of an aesthetic that systematically reinforces the discipline of desire that supports industrial

---

a circular relation and interchange between irreducibly conflicting practices, between a *disciplinary* control of the body and a *deployment of sexuality* and desire (pp. 139 et passim)—the circuit that I am calling a *discipline of desire*. I will be returning to this double discourse of power in the following chapters.

52. Stuart Ewen, *Captains of Consciousness: Advertising and the Social Roots of the Consumer Culture* (New York: McGraw-Hill, 1976), 61.

capitalism. Advertising, as one of its earliest theorists put it, is "the art of creating a want."[53] Far from imposing a puritanical censorship, the art of advertising manifestly solicits desire: advertising, a contributor to the *Encyclopaedia of the Social Sciences* (1922) observed, "is almost the only force at work against puritanism in consumption. It can infuse art into the things of life; and it will."[54] It is the art of something better: "rightfully applied, [advertising] is the method by which the desire is created for better things."[55]

Nor does the discourse of advertising merely "coopt" James's imagined resistances to capitalist power. Rather, the appeal of an advertising aesthetic is already implicit in James's own fictional practice. " 'It's an art like another, and infinite like all the arts,' " Chad says of the "art of advertising" at the close of *The Ambassadors*: "Advertising scientifically worked presented itself thus as the great new force. 'It really does the thing, you know.' " Strether's skepticism toward Chad's claims is clear enough, but in fact Strether's own actions in the novel have been nothing but a testimony to the power of advertisement. When Chad states that advertising "really does the thing," Strether asks: "Affects, you mean, the sale of the object advertised?" Chad replies: "Yes—but it affects it extraordinarily; really beyond what one had supposed." Advertising goes "beyond" a mere affect on sales because it alters the very status of the desired object. The advertising spectacle does not simply represent (or misrepresent) the object; it does not simply supplement what Strether calls the "real thing." Rather, it affirms the representation as the thing desired: as Guy Debord puts it, "considered in its own terms, the spectacle is the *affirmation* of appearance and the affirmation of all human, namely social life, as mere appear-

53. Thomas Herbert Russell, *Advertising: Methods and Mediums* (Chicago: International Business Library, 1910), 268.

54. Leverett S. Lyon, "Advertising," in *The Encylopaedia of the Social Sciences* Vol. 1 (1922), 475.

55. Calvin Coolidge, as cited by Frank S. Presbrey, *The History and Development of Advertising* (New York: Doubleday, Doran, 1929), 622.

ance."[56] And Strether, despite his insistent search for the "real thing" beneath the Parisian world of appearances, takes Chad, the master of appearance, as the model of his desires. Chad is "formed to please," and this form provides the spectacular representation of Strether's wants: "Oh, Chad!—it was that rare youth he should have enjoyed being 'like.'" Chad himself functions as an advertisement for Strether, as an ad for the freedom and youth he has missed. And *The Ambassadors* comprehensively testifies to a power of representatives and surrogates of desire that is nothing but the power of advertisement. Advertising, "in the hands, naturally, of a master [the Master?]..., *c'est un monde.*"[57]

---

56. Guy Debord, *The Society of the Spectacle* (Detroit, 1970), para. 10.

57. Henry James, *The Ambassadors* (New York: Scribner's, 1909), 2:315, 316 (vol. 22 of the New York Edition).

4

Images of the Opposite: The Aesthetic Rewriting of Power

On every level, the techniques of resistance that James devises in his fiction and in *The American Scene* turn out to be versions of the very technologies of power that he ostensibly disavows. The forms and deformations of the Jamesian text are radically entangled with the technologies of power. It is this "same criminal continuity" between art and power that is the artfully dissembled secret of James's art. That art, in its very resistances to power, is an art of power. I noted earlier that *The American Scene* participates in a general social movement of professionalization and that part of this movement involves a partitioning and segregation of disciplines and discourses, the demarcation of exclusive domains of expertise. When James in one of his prefaces, for instance, speaks of a "created expertness," he is referring both to his own policies of representation and to the expertise that these policies authorize and produce in his readers.[1]

Jamesian criticism has displayed such an expertness, in the formalizing of novelistic and critical practices, and perhaps above all in its moves to free the novel from the claims of rival

---

1. Henry James, Preface to "The Aspern Papers," in *The Art of the Novel* (New York: Scribner's, 1934), 177.

discourses and disciplines. But every disciplinary formation is also a policing action, and it should by now be clear that the attempt to escape the shame of power is itself political. This is, I think, the dissimulated lesson of the Master, a lesson almost unreadable if only because we have so thoroughly kept up the blind that James himself put in place, have averted scandal by enforcing a break between literary discourse and the discourses of power. Reinforcing the Jamesian ruse, James's critics have read him as the very exemplar of an aesthetic outside the circuit of power. I have been arguing that this ruse is itself the ruse of power.

The present study can serve only as an introduction to a much larger investigation of the links between the art of the novel and the subject of power. But it is necessary to indicate the direction that I think this investigation should take and also what is entailed by the analytics of power that I have been proposing. More precisely, it is necessary to ask what follows from the Foucauldian view of the politics of the novel that I have been setting out.

I

One way of clarifying what is involved here is by returning to James's reading of Washington in *The American Scene*. Particularly interesting about James's account of the nation's political capital, it will be recalled, is the radical displacement or "general elimination" of the signs of power. If in *The Princess Casamassima* and in *The Golden Bowl* power appears where it can hardly be suspected, in *The American Scene* the nominal or official site of power presents only a vague blank. One might say that at the close of the Washington chapter, James engages in an attempt to "see" power, and this attempt is perverse on at least two counts: first, because, as I have been arguing all along, power is a relational and not a substantial construct—a field of relations—and second, because it is the dissemination and distribution of the political throughout the social body that James's texts trace. Power is embedded in the ensemble of social networks, not merely or even primarily in those institutions officially designated as political. These power relations, we have noted, centrally involve a nexus of visibility and invisibility, of blindness and surveillance. But power scarcely appears as such.

More significant, however, is the form the displacement of power takes in *The American Scene.* I have argued that the Jamesian text displays a criminal continuity between art and power, but the perfect fit between aesthetic and political forms in the Washington chapter, and in *The American Scene* generally, perhaps reveals something more. The exact equivalence of art and power that James represents here achieves in fact an emptying out of the category of the political and an ultimate reabsorption of the political within the bounds of "the literary." It is as if power has become merely a metaphor for the art of the novel. Another way of saying this is that if art and power become synonymous or reversible terms in *The American Scene,* James's practice ultimately points to a comprehensive aestheticizing of power. The sovereign primacy of art is paradoxically reaffirmed, not by disavowing the political—as in *The Princess Casamassima* or in *The Golden Bowl*—but instead by embracing the continuity between art and power. Far from disowning power, *The American Scene* aesthetically reappropriates the political. What can this aestheticizing of power tell us about the politics of the novel?

The double discourse of the Jamesian text makes for what might be called crises of equivalence. The tautological relation of vision and supervision in *The Princess Casamassima,* of love and regulation in *The Golden Bowl,* of art and power in *The American Scene* constitutes a two-tiered writing: on one level, an aesthetic resistance to the exercises of power, on another, a discreet reinscription of strategies of control. This double discourse does not indicate an "ambiguity" or "undecidability" about the status of power in the novel. Rather, it enables the institution of the novel to act as a relay of mechanisms of social control at the same time that it protects itself against the shame of power. The novel, above all, engages in an aesthetic rewriting of power. Even as it speaks out against systems of coercion, the novel reinvents them and makes them acceptable in another form, in the form of the novel itself.

Art and power are not at odds in the novel; opposed from one point of view, they are in fact arranged like the two "sides" of a horseshoe. The nineteenth-century novel accomplishes a comprehensive reappropriation or rewriting of power, the aestheticizing of power that *The American Scene* enacts in such an exemplary and almost diagrammatic fashion. We might consider, for example, Zola's importation into the novel of economic, medical, industrial, and political discourses; Dreiser's or Norris's narratives of force, mappings of the links between capitalism and desire, between novelistic techniques of representation and financial, scientific, and sexual constructions of the self and of the social body; or, in a different form, Henry Adams's devising of an art of power in the *Education,* a text in which force and aesthetics are progressively incorporated. The novel does not simply enlarge its field of documentation or simply "reflect" social regimes of power and knowledge. What one reads here is an aesthetic reinscription of power within the ostensibly "powerless" discourse of the novel, an aesthetic translation of power that supplements and extends social networks of policing and regulation. Put simply, the novel makes power acceptable in the form of the aesthetic representation itself. If the novel appropriates the underworld of crime and policing as a literary entertainment, if the novel rewrites strategies of supervision and normalization as the aesthetic proprieties of omniscient narration and organic form, if the novel's techniques of representation are shot through with social technologies of power, then far from being at odds, art and power are simply inseparable.

Hence the point is not to read the novel in terms of a power that lies beyond or outside it; power is already immanent in the novel. Now Foucault's analyses have emphasized the links between political and discursive practices. Speech does not merely verbalize or represent conflict and domination, Foucault argues, it is the very object of conflict; the exercising of power cannot be separated from the deployment and control of discourse. The aesthetic rewriting of power involves such a struggle for control over discourse. In *Surveiller et punir*, for instance, Foucault comments on the emergence of a "whole new literature of crime" at the close of the eighteenth century. The new literature displaces the popular stories and broadsheets that had "formed part of the basic reading of the lower classes." This popular literature was a "two-sided" writing, at once indicting and glorifying the lower-class criminal, ironically justifying the criminality it brought to justice. The new crime and detection stories undo this ironic dissent. Exploiting an aesthetics of crime—murder considered as one of the fine arts—the "high" literature achieves an aesthetic appropriation of criminality, effectively relegating the details of everyday criminality to the unheroic and subliterary newspapers. But if by mid-century the "great murders had become the quiet game of the well behaved," this game is also ideologically two-sided. If the older stories incited the very illegalities they were avowedly directed against, the literature that supplants them "inaugurated the theoretical play of an illegality of the privileged; or rather it marked the moment when the political and economic illegalities actually practiced by the bourgeoisie were to be duplicated in theoretical and aesthetic representation." The aesthetic representation of criminality thus transposes the "privilege" of crime to another social group and appropriates the discourse of criminality in the interests of that group.[2]

The traditional novel's treatment of the crime of power, we have seen, displays a similar two-sidedness, and if the novel duplicates power relations in another form, such an aesthetic duplication serves political interests. But to say this is clearly not to propose a "theory" of power in the novel. I noted at the outset that the attempt to theorize the base of historical or political

---

2. Michel Foucault, *Discipline and Punish: The Birth of the Prison*, trans. Alan Sheridan (New York: Pantheon, 1977), 68–69, 285.

knowledge—the attempt to ground interpretation outside or beneath the risks of practice—expresses a desire to escape an inevitable politics of interpretation. The desire for a theory that can predict or govern action or interpretation from the outside manifests above all a fear of power. The Foucauldian account of power discourse relations that I have been endorsing centrally indicates the always unstable or ironic, always reversible, ultimately ungovernable and unpredictable resistances and countereffects of the aesthetic rewriting of power. The novel represents and supplements the increasing "disciplining" of modern Western society since the late eighteenth century. The novel participates in what Foucault has called "the increasingly better invigilated process of adjustment . . . between productive activities, resources of communication, and the play of power-relations" that modern society has sought after.[3] But if James's texts, for instance, display an "adjustment" of the novel to discourses of power, these texts also indicate that such coordinations and adjustments are neither uniform nor constant. Power requires and bends resistances, but this is not a zero-sum game; in Foucault's terms, "in a given society, there is no general type of equilibrium" between discursive and political practices.[4]

In a recent critique of Foucault from a Marxist perspective, Frank Lentricchia has pointed to Foucault's refusal "to theorize" power relations "within a larger historical narrative of relations of exploitation."[5] Crucially, the desire for theory is also a desire for a grand narrative. As Fredric Jameson expresses it, literary history must be "retold within the unity of a single great collective story . . . as vital episodes in a single vast unfinished plot."[6] Foucault's local and empirical narratives indeed refuse the the-

---

3. Michel Foucault, "The Subject and Power," *Critical Inquiry* 8 (Summer 1982), 788.

4. Foucault, "The Subject and Power," 787. For an important critique of the claims of literary theory, see Steven Knapp and Walter Benn Michaels, "Against Theory," *Critical Inquiry* 8 (Summer 1982), 723–42.

5. Frank Lentricchia, "Reading Foucault (1)," *Raritan* 1 (Spring 1982), 20.

6. Fredric Jameson, *The Political Unconscious* (Ithaca: Cornell University Press, 1981), 19, 20.

oretical unity of a single narrative. But this constitutes, I think, just the strength of the account he offers. The form of power relations is neither inevitable nor univocal, and the novel does not tell a single story of power. The only inevitability is that our interpretation and appropriation of texts—including of course my own reading of the novel—will remain political, and the theoretical move to escape from the impositions of power, interest, and belief is neither possible nor desirable.

II

Clearly, however, the detailed rituals of power that Foucault traces in modern Western society—and that, I have been arguing, are promoted by the institution of the novel itself—have a specific coherence. The policing of the real, the optics of surveillance and discipline, the biopolitics of the family, the great and small political technologies of normalization and regulation: all are inscribed in the novel in the form of a *dispositif,* or "grid of intelligibility," that it has been possible to read. I have emphasized the recalcitrant heterogeneity and dispersion of modern power relations, relations that, as Foucault maintains, include "discourses, institutions, architectural forms, regulatory decisions, laws, administrative measures, scientific statements, philosophical moral and philanthropic propositions."[7] I have tried to specify the grid on which these practices of power, knowledge, and discourse cross. What must be emphasized is that this heterogeneous domain is not a "unity" guaranteed by suprahistorical rules that transcend these local practices or by underlying laws that govern the stages of a yet-unfinished movement to the completion and resolution of a "single plot."

---

7. Michel Foucault, "The Confession of the Flesh," in *Power/Knowledge: Selected Interviews and Other Writings by Michel Foucault, 1972–1977,* ed. Colin Gordon (New York: Pantheon, 1980), 194.

Disciplinary power inheres in the practices and relations that constitute it; power does not rule "from the outside."

Hence social practices do not merely "represent" power; they are in fact what they appear to be.[8] This is perhaps the central difference between a Foucauldian and Marxian accounts of power relations—a difference between what might be called an avowedly "superficial" reading and a deep reading of social forms as reflections, manifestations, or symptoms of a latent content. It is worth reiterating some of the other differences. Again, the relational character of power exchanges means that power is exercised and not owned. This of course does not mean one cannot define strategic "positions" of domination. But it does suggest that the notion that power is only or even primarily applied by those at the top to those at the bottom is finally illusory. As Foucault describes the panoptic technology, for example, "the most diabolical aspect of the idea and of all the applications it brought about" is its diffused, anonymous, and reciprocal—though always asymmetrical—operation: "In this form of management, power is not totally entrusted to someone who would exercise it alone, over others, in an absolute fashion; rather this machine is one in which everyone is caught, those who exercise this power, as well as those who are subjected to it."[9] These reciprocally coercive operations of power make it necessary to revise traditional oppositions of hegemony and margin, law and transgression, power and resistance—and, collaterally, make it necessary to revise the virtually automatic reading of "the literary" as subversive, marginal, and transgressive, as essentially opposed to the political.

Normalizing arrangements of power, we have seen, succeed by never *quite* succeeding. The goal is not to eliminate offenses

---

8. I am indebted here to Hubert L. Dreyfus and Paul Rabinow, *Michel Foucault: Beyond Structuralism and Hermeneutics* (Chicago: University of Chicago Press, 1982), 109, 110.

9. Michel Foucault, "The Eye of Power," in *Power/Knowledge*, ed. Gordon, 156. I quote here from the translation of the passage in Dreyfus and Rabinow, *Michel Foucault*, 192.

and infractions but to "use" them: "to assimilate the transgression of the laws in a general tactics of subjection."[10] The achievement of normalizing arrangements is this *coupling* of power and resistance. Not merely tolerating but requiring resistances, not merely controlling and classifying but also creating and producing the abnormalities, anomalies, and delinquencies that extend the range of its operations. We must contrast here the view of power as essentially or exclusively negative, censoring, and repressive—what Foucault calls, in *La Volonté de savoir*, the "repressive hypothesis"—and a view of power as productive and even creative. Crucially, the spread of normalizing strategies entails the production of abnormalities that must then be known, ordered, supervised, and reformed; and in this way, knowledge, discourse, and power are linked and extended into larger and larger fields. Seen in this way, what Raymond Williams has described as the novel's aspiration for "knowable community" takes on a markedly different significance.

The novel participates in this normalizing movement, and as a form and as an institution takes part in the practical and theoretical search for supervisory and regulative tactics. The double discourse of the novel, we have seen, has the double movement of an inoculative operation. It is tempting to read this double discourse as an ambivalent or ambiguous writing, as an inherently indecisive writing that produces, through its very indecisions, an internal and critical distance from power and ideology. That is, it is tempting to discover in the doubleness of the novel an ironic and ironizing resistance, intrinsic to the literary itself, that subverts the impositions of power.[11]

One problem with such a reading, however, is that it ignores or represses the two-sidedness of modern power relations themselves: the forms of modern power, it might be said, are themselves structured ironically. And this irony of power makes it necessary to reconsider the role played by the ironic and am-

10. Foucault, *Discipline and Punish*, 272.
11. For a provocative statement of this position, see Leo Bersani, "The Subject of Power," *Diacritics* 7:3 (1977), 11–12.

bivalent structures of "the literary"—as they have been institutionalized and critically reproduced—in rendering acceptable the art of power itself. We might reconsider how the ritualized readings of the novel, in the family parlor, the study, and the school, have worked to domesticate, rewrite, and render normal the very normalizing moves of power that the literary text has been taken to resist.

James's texts provide an exemplary display of this reinvention of power. The intent here has not been to survey the range of James's texts nor even to indicate an "evolution" of James's representation of the subject of power. Rather, I have pointed to an ensemble of insistences in James's work and a certain trajectory—a formalizing of what I have referred to as the "rules" for representing power in the novel and the devising of increasingly discreet and immanent forms of regulation. One might trace this trajectory from Roderick Hudson's early and conspicuous protest: "What I resent is that the range of your vision should pretend to be the limit of my action."[12] If this protest names the linkage of vision and supervision that defines, for instance, the literature of detection, there is clearly a reworking of this too-obvious network of seeing and power, from the early fiction, through the foregrounded fantasy of surveillance that *The Princess Casamassima* at once invokes and disavows, to the reinscription of policing in the discreet vigilance of the later fiction. Moreover, one of the things that attracted James to the drama and attracted him despite the broad critique of the theater in *The Tragic Muse* (itself virtually an inventory of aesthetic and political modes of representation, and their entanglement) was that the drama forced the novelist to devise a comprehensive internalization of supervision. The drama provided a model of "self-regulation" that dispensed with narratorial surveillance and inscribed control in characters ostensibly "standing on their own feet and going of themselves." Disowning regulation and securing it at another level, the dramatic mode thus provided a model

---

12. Henry James, *Roderick Hudson* (New York: Scribner's, 1907), 504.

for the organic and immanent policing that invests James's late fiction.

Something more is involved here, however, than the devising of more and more tactful tactics of regulation. Modern political technologies, we have seen, justify themselves through an unceasing reinscription of power in nominally nonpolitical systems. James's texts display such a dispersion and displacement of power relations. This is clearest in what I have described as the *tautological* relations of seeing and overseeing, love and vigilance, discourse and power in James's work. Just as the happy family and prison are suspended in relation to each other in the Philadelphia section of *The American Scene,* just as *The Golden Bowl* displays a paradoxical economy of care and supervision, the Jamesian text projects the pseudoalternatives of a tautology: the double discourse of the novel suspends apparently opposed terms in relation to each other. The novel projects, to paraphrase James, "images of the opposite" that are in fact two ways of saying the same thing.[13] This double discourse has been at once acknowledged and repressed in Jamesian criticism, and there has been a critical tendency to rewrite these tautological relations as a radical opposition or polarization—in the broadest terms, as a radical opposition between aesthetics and politics that James has been taken to define.

An apparently very different but in fact closely allied move has been to rewrite the Jamesian suspension or tautology as an intrinsic undecidability or "ambiguity"—the key word that at once names and screens the criminal continuities of the Jamesian work. What has been taken to define the novels immediately preceding the "major phase," for instance—novels such as *What Maisie Knew, The Awkward Age, The Turn of the Screw,* and *The Sacred Fount*—has been, of course, an irreducible ambiguity. James indeed explicitly invites such a reading, and the Jamesian text insists on the ambiguities and tensions that, I suggest, at once produce and contain the apparently dispersive and subver-

---

13. I am paraphrasing James's Preface to *The Golden Bowl,* in *The Art of the Novel,* 343.

sive elements of the novel. James advertises, for example, the
bewilderment and "muddle" of *What Maisie Knew,* a text that
enacts the transformation of sex into discourse in the form of a
prurient innocence; he foregrounds the "fruits of compromise"
and "consequent muddle," the entanglement of innocence and
exploitation—of "taking up" and "letting alone"—that centers
The Awkward Age's drama of freedom and appropriation; he
invokes, in *The Ambassadors,* similar polarities of "interpretative
innocence" and violation, of "touching" and "not touching."[14]
These sustained and muddled polarities cover the interdependent and finally tautological relation of the images of the opposite in the Jamesian text. What they all but acknowledge—as
an unreadable ambiguity or absurd confusion—are the inex-
tricably related and imbricated moves of appropriation, knowledge, and desire that traverse the Jamesian text.

I have already suggested, to take another instance, that *The
Turn of the Screw* tells a story something like the story of love and
power told by *The Golden Bowl.* Not merely does the governess,
in her roles of tutor, nurse, confessor, and analyst, occupy in
turn the power roles of the "medico-tutelary complex," but
more significantly, the text's incitements to "know" are throughout bound up with the excitations and pleasures of the "power-
knowledge" nexus that informs James's late texts. Further, to
the extent that *The Turn of the Screw* has come to emblematize
Jamesian "ambiguity," it is possible to say that the advertised
ambiguities of the story—the undecidable "choice" between
ghost and madness narratives, however taken up—have worked
to displace, by repeating in another register, this inside—or perhaps too-evident—story of desire, knowledge, and power.

I am suggesting then that the "aesthetic" production of iron-
ies, tensions, and ambiguities in the Jamesian text ultimately
serves the authority and interests that these signs of "liter-

---

14. James, *The Awkward Age* (New York: Penguin, 1977), 190–91; Preface to
The Awkward Age, 105, Preface to *The Ambassadors,* 324, both in *The Art of the
Novel; The Ambassadors* (New York: Scribner's, 1907), 2:271 (vol. 22 of the New
York Edition).

ariness" have generally been seen to question or even to subvert. The reason is not merely that, as in the case of the novels of the 1890s, narratives of power have been rewritten, and depoliticized, as "purely" or "merely" epistemological exercises.[15] More significant, the aesthetic and theoretical disavowal of the double discourse of power has been supported by the virtually automatic and still-dominant conception of "the literary" as subversive, resistant, and liberating.

To take a recent and important instance, John Carlos Rowe, in *Through the Custom-House: Nineteenth-Century American Fiction and Modern Theory*, appeals throughout to what he sees as the violently disruptive and subversive character of literary language. Focusing on "marginal" and "eccentric" texts, Rowe takes as his governing premise "the subversive impulse of literature in general" and endorses the "general conception of literary language as the violation of the normative."[16] Not surprisingly, this model of the literary as fundamentally subversive goes hand in hand with a model of power as fundamentally repressive. Hence for Rowe, what literature exposes are "the various repressions at work in different cultural codes," and what the literary performs is a "subversion of the normative that liberates the social signified."[17]

If such an arrangement guarantees an absolute antinomy between the literary and the political, the subversive and the repressive, this deceptive symmetry, I have been arguing, also works to protect and to provide the alibi for the very structures of power that Rowe sees the literary—and literary theory—as undermining. Alternatively we might say that Rowe's account ends up reaffirming the very normative scenario that it imagines itself undoing and leaves in place the ideological oppositions

---

15. See, for instance, Manfred Mackenzie, *Communities of Honor and Love in Henry James* (Cambridge: Harvard University Press, 1976), 22; Ora Segal, *The Lucid Reflector: The Observer in Henry James's Fiction* (New Haven: Yale University Press, 1969), 169.

16. John Carlos Rowe, *Through the Custom-House* (Baltimore: Johns Hopkins University Press, 1982), 17, 10.

17. Ibid., 9, 187.

that it purports to question. For our purposes, Rowe's reading of James's *The Sacred Fount* provides a convenient instance of this ultimately normalizing gesture of violation, resistance, and liberation, a gesture that has been repeated frequently in recent literary theory.

For one thing, despite the crucial observation that "self-consciousness still preserves its romantic status as a liberation from social confinement and historical determination," Rowe, at least in his account of *The Sacred Fount*, essentially endorses this romantic and liberating view, asserting that the narrator achieves authenticity—"discovers himself"—by "undermining his own authority" through an imaginative and "critical self-consciousness." Rowe here draws not merely on de Man's notion of the literary as valorized by its self-deconstructing character but also on a version of what Foucault has critically described as an "analytic of finitude": put simply, the belief that becoming conscious of the social and political determinants of the self and world liberates one from these determinants.[18] The "desire for freedom" that Rowe attributes to the narrator and the novel both is above all a desire to escape from the inevitable interests and enforcements that produce meaning. This escape takes the form of a self-conscious discovery, or rather "rediscovery of the arbitrariness of the sign." And this arbitrariness of the sign, Rowe insists, destabilizes every attempt to enclose meaning within a system or structure of authority. According to a model we have already examined, the literary is thus seen to resist the impositions both of meaning and of power, to resist by way of a "politics" founded on a theory of signification: the arbitrariness of the sign.

This is not the place to consider this highly dubious, and often repeated, rewriting of a linguistic as a political arbitrariness, but it is not hard to see the appeal of the illegitimate allegorizing of a general theory of language as a theory of power and liberation.[19] For now, it is worth recalling that Rowe, in his earlier

---

18. Ibid., 171, 168.

Henry Adams and Henry James, had argued that what defines the literary is that it gives form to the essentially formless, chaotic, and "infinite muddle" of actuality, that it provides a "formal enclosure" for an essentially formless reality. In his more recent *Through the Custom-House,* the relation between art and world has been inverted. Thus, the role of the literary is to "question the enclosing forms which constitute social authority." Invoking a familiar polarity, Rowe argues that the narrator "discloses an open language" in the process of subverting the "closed society of Newmarch."[20]

What is clearest about these reversible oppositions is the critic's eagerness to define the literary as the reverse of the political and thus to posit the freedom and resistant autonomy of the literary. This desire is not unlike the Marxian eagerness to posit and embrace utopian scenarios, the desire "to wrest a realm of Freedom from a realm of Necessity."[21] Clearly, such formulations idealize and authorize the very oppositions in question; and the utopian desire for a freestanding and autonomous literary discourse reinvokes the fantasies of an autonomous self and of a (literary) world elsewhere while leaving untouched and in fact idealizing the political systems it would escape.

Rowe's account of *The Sacred Fount* again makes this gesture emphatically clear. "The narrator's theory" of signification, Rowe argues, "subverts the very illusion of social order" supported by Obert's "official" art. But social order, although constructed, is hardly illusory, and only the illusion that it is produces the notion that theory can subvert it or escape from it. The narrator, it will be recalled, is finally expelled from Newmarch, expelled as a madman: "My poor dear, you are crazy, and good night." Rowe insists that this expulsion be read as a

---

19. See, for instance, Barbara Johnson, *The Critical Difference* (Baltimore: Johns Hopkins University Press, 1980), esp. chap. 6, "Melville's Fist: The Execution of *Billy Budd,*" for such a "political" allegory of reading.

20. Rowe, *Henry Adams and Henry James* (Ithaca: Cornell University Press, 1976), 159; *Through the Custom-House,* 187, 188.

21. Fredric Jameson, *The Political Unconscious,* 19.

liberating escape from the normative scenario of Newmarch and asserts that the narrator has somehow "prepared for" this expulsion from "society." But for James this escape from society is quite literally utopian: the word that casts out the narrator is a "word that put me altogether nowhere."[22] And his expulsion, far from undermining the normative, achieves in fact a twofold reaffirmation of the norm.

Within the novel, the banishment of the narrator as mad explicitly reconfirms the ruling "tone" of Newmarch; and the novel itself, as Rowe's own account richly displays, effects a segregation of the literary from the shame of power that trivializes the power of social order even as it leaves that order intact. The novel stages a utopian fantasy of the freestanding self and of an autonomous discourse and invites an aesthetic and theoretical rewriting of power; the Jamesian text, as we have seen, invites a critical reading that repeats the very normalizing operations that the text at once identifies and secures.

Put somewhat differently, the view of the novel, and of the literary in general, as intrinsically ironic and subversive is part of a comprehensive suppression of the internal relations between power and discourse in modern society. The very notion of knowledge and discourse as exterior to the political, Foucault has shown, has become the general form of power's acceptability. If power merely silences and represses, knowledge and discourse speak the truth that sets one free; and the repressive hypothesis covers for this entanglement between discourse and power. Modern strategies of regulation screen themselves by producing "oppositional" discourses that in fact form part of a larger deployment of power. I want to close this chapter by examining how the production of what has been taken as an autonomous literary discourse entails such a double agency.

---

22. Rowe, *Through the Custom-House*, 185, 187; *The Sacred Fount* (New York: Scribner's, 1901), 318, 319.

III

"There are two values of literary work—distinct, separate, not commensurable," Walter Besant observes in his auto-biographical account of the formation of the Society of Authors, founded in 1880. The first is what Besant calls the "literary value" of a work, the value that defines the "real position" of the writer. But the problem is that this real value has become "confused" with another value that is, according to Besant, entirely distinct—the monetary value, or "the price it will command; and this price cannot be measured by the literary or artistic value." Such a distinction between literary and market values is, of course, familiar enough and might indeed be read as one of the defining oppositions of the modernist aesthetic. For the moment, what is particularly interesting are the reasons that Besant, among others, gives for this "confusion of ideas between literary and commercial value." Why has the confusion appeared, and what purpose might it serve?[23]

Besant distinguishes between two stages of literary "production" to ground these two distinct values. "While an artist is at work upon a poem, a drama, or a romance," he insists, "this aspect of his work, and this alone, is in his mind, otherwise his work would be naught. But once finished and ready for production, then comes in the other value—the commercial value, which is a distinct thing. Here the artist ceases and the man of business begins."[24] Besant fails to clarify this mysterious transition, or rather break, between the artist and the man of business. What is essential, in his account, is that neither producer—the man of business or the man of letters—infiltrate and vitiate the other.[25]

23. Walter Besant, *Autobiography of Sir Walter Besant* (New York: Dodd, Mead, 1902), 227, 228.

24. Besant, *Autobiography*, 227–28.

25. My account here is directly indebted to John Goode, "The Decadent Writer as Producer," in *Decadence and the 1890s* ed. Ian Fletcher (Stratford-upon-Avon Studies, 17, 1979; reprint New York, 1980). On the literary marketplace,

But if Besant insists on the incommensurability of these two positions and these two values, the role of the Society of Authors itself contributed to their conflation or confusion. For one thing, the society centrally promoted the more general movement of literary professionalization in the later nineteenth century, not merely in its campaign for the international copyright agreement (passed in 1891, the same year that the society founded its professional journal, *The Author*), nor merely in its sponsoring of "how to" books such as S. Squire Sprigge's *Methods of Publishing* (1890). More significant here is the notion of the literary text that the society produced and endorsed.

The primary objective of the Society of Authors was "the maintenance, definition, and defence of literary property." And crucially, this view of literature as a form of property, protected by copyright law—the governing view of literature as an exchangeable commodity—is seen to be disturbingly at odds with the distinct literary value that the society worked to protect. The initial chapter of Sprigge's *Methods*, for instance, is called "literary property," and the central claim is that a "man's literary work is, though the fact is too often forgotten, his personal property, which he may use absolutely as he chooses, over which he alone has control, to sell, to lend, to give away."[26] Sprigge implicitly distinguishes between "personal" and "public" property, between the author's free use and control of his work and the market production or publication that follows upon his artistic production. Sprigge thus distinguishes, along the same lines as Besant, between what might be called the intrinsic (literary) and extrinsic (commercial) properties of the text. But it is not hard to see that this free use and control is in fact illusory, since the only control that Sprigge acknowledges is precisely a choice

---

in addition to the sources already cited, see: Christopher P. Wilson, "American Naturalism and the Problem of Sincerity," *American Literature* 54 (December 1982), 511–27; Walter Benn Michaels, "Dreiser's *Financier*: The Man of Business as a Man of Letters," in *American Realism: New Essays*, ed. Eric J. Sundquist (Baltimore: Johns Hopkins University Press, 1982), 278–95.

26. S. Squire Sprigge, *Methods of Publishing* (London, 1890), 113, 9.

of ways to give over that control ("to sell, to lend, to give away"). We might say that the author's only power, in this account, is his power to withhold the text from the process of production and circulation. But this dubious power would not merely deny the author the benefits of his production, and of a readership; it would also directly contradict the society's definition of the work as property: property is simply not property at all *unless* it can be exchanged or alienated.

I am suggesting that the society's program is inherently contradictory. The attempt is to formulate an alternative to the exchange of the work as a commodity, as a book within the economic practices of book production. But what these writers construct is an illusory area of freedom from the market that their own professionalizing initatives explicitly undermine. Moreover, it might be said that the former is an attempt to screen and compensate for the latter: the production of the notion of an autonomous literary text and of an intrinsic literary value is the production of an image of the opposite, an image that screens the thorough inscription of the text within the property relations of the market.

The radical break between two conceptions of the author (the man of letters and the man of business), between two distinct "economies" (what James called the "sublime economy" of literary form and the market economy of publication), between, in general terms, intrinsic and extrinsic determinations of the text and of textual value: these are the antinomies invoked in the general nineteenth-century reorganization of discursive practices, and of course the oppositions that continue to govern large areas of literary criticism and literary theory. They are also the antinomies that structure James's stories of writers and artists in the 1880s and 1890s, and returning to James can perhaps clarify what is at stake here. "The Death of the Lion," for instance, a story that originally appeared in *The Yellow Book* in 1894, centers on what the narrator at least sees as the radical incompatibility between professional and artistic interests, "two interests . . . in their essence opposed." Personal, private, aesthetic imperatives

are arrayed against "professional flair" and the commercial interests of the public and of publication.[27]

But from the start, the narrator's own story, in order to exist
at all, acknowledges the need to violate just this essential opposition: "These meagre notes are essentially private," he declares,
"so that if they see the light the insidious forces that, *as my story
itself shows,* make at present for publicity, will simply have over-
mastered my precautions." Indeed, the story itself shows that
the forces of publicity cannot be seen as merely external to the
literary text. The narrator, like Besant and Sprigge, posits an
ultimately illusory private space, free from the market, to save
the text from its fate as a commodity. This free space is again
located between authorial and commercial production. It takes
the form of an anachronistic manuscript circulation by means of
which both author and text "circulated in person." The text is
thus given, to adapt John Goode's formulation, "a magical ability to operate in a phase of circulation before it becomes a commodity."[28] But this ability turns out to be, on both sides, a lia-
bility in the story. The circulation of the author, in person,
transforms *him* into a commodity—the "lion" or literary celebri-
ty—and the circulation of the manuscript from hand to hand
inevitably leads to its irrecoverable loss. The double discourse of
"The Death of the Lion" hence at once promotes and undoes an
essential opposition between aesthetic and professional interests.
James's story represents complex relations of authorship, death,
and textuality, but at least one of its messages is unequivocal:
one cannot eliminate the market without eliminating the work of
literature itself.

My brief discussion of the shifting relations between literature
and the market can merely point to the larger history of literary
professionalization in the nineteenth century and the progressive production of the institution of the literary. But this

27. Henry James, "The Death of the Lion," in *Novels and Tales of Henry James,*
The New York Edition, 24 vols. (New York: Scribner's, 1909), 15:124, 102.
28. James, "The Death of the Lion," 103, 122; John Goode, "The Decadent
Writer as Producer," 119.

discussion is perhaps enough to indicate that movements of literary professionalization do not simply compromise or threaten the intrinsic, aesthetic value of the text. On the contrary, the notion of the "literary" as an autonomous, specialized, and demarcated discursive practice is at least in part *produced* by this professionalization and indeed *required* as its counter-image. Moreover, the "entire independence" of the literary that Besant contradictorily declares is not simply a mystification. We must examine how this contradiction and difference between literary and worldly initiatives may be brought to function within a larger discourse of power. I will be returning to this topic of literary difference in the next chapter, but for now I want to indicate how such a notion of difference functions in James's late work.

Not surprisingly, the production of this view of "the literary"—of an ivory tower aesthetic—is the subject of James's unfinished novel, *The Ivory Tower*. *The Ivory Tower* displays not merely the double discourse of disavowal and reinscription that, as we have seen, characterizes the Jamesian text; it displays as well the way in which the notion of an autonomous literary discourse is underwritten by and supports the very power—what James here calls the "force of the money-power"—that the literary is seen as writing against.[29] *The Ivory Tower* takes as its always displaced and suppressed subject the criminal continuity between art and power that I have been tracing, and it will thus provide a closing image of the Jamesian art of power.

In the surviving plan for *The Ivory Tower*, James is obligingly straightforward about what Graham Fiedler is intended to represent in the novel: "I have always wanted to do an out and out non-producer, in the ordinary sense of non-accumulator of material gain" (pp. 336–337). James can here equate production and accumulation, or rather nonproduction and nonaccumulation, because Gray is to represent a total rejection and negation

29. Henry James, *"The Ivory Tower" and "Notes for 'The Ivory Tower'"* (New York: Scribner's, 1917), 317. Subsequent references to the novel and to the notes in this edition appear in parentheses in the text.

of market relations. Gray is to be "as different as possible" from the inhabitants of the American world of ferocious acquisition; he is to be a sort of "floating island" of "'culture'" (p. 338). And his "entire difference" is made possible by the real absence, or more precisely, what James calls the "real suppression for him of anything that shall count in the American air as a money-making" desire or knowledge (p. 336). James's novel explicitly takes as its subject what it "doesn't *know*" or refuses to know and, embracing this ignorance of power, makes the "absence of it" into the very "core of the subject" (pp. 296, 294, 293). In *The Ivory Tower*, that is, the censorship or suppression of the subject of power becomes in fact the novel's subject.

The novel is obsessively drawn to what it works to suppress, and the disavowal of the money-power and money-passion is linked throughout to another and related suppression. Outlining the relation between Horty Vint and Cissy Foy in his notes for the novel, for instance, James observes that "in a world of money they can't *not* go in for it, and that accordingly so long as neither has it, they can't go in for each other" (p. 301). There is a precise equivalence and exchangeability implied here between monetary and sexual relations, and indeed Cissy Foy functions in the novel as a kind of "shifter" between these two related and displaced passions. The projected plot becomes literally a matter of "marrying money" (p. 302)—or of renouncing love and money both. And Cissy becomes a register both of an innocence and of a suppressed and evaded experience and knowledge that James all but refuses to name. "Though I want her a Girl," James writes, "I want her not too young a one either. Everything about her, her intelligence, character, sense of life and knowledge of it, imply a certain experience and a certain time for that" (p. 298). James simply leaves it at *that,* but his narrative incites a prurient fascination with this "knowledge" and with the Girl's "mysterious" character—a desire to know, for example, about her relations with Gray's step-father, "a person . . . to whom she has been somehow very 'nice'" (p. 298).

James's narratives typically provoke interest in what they censor and disavow, and the double omission of power and sexuality, the twin denial of "knowledge," becomes a compulsive and compelling silence in the text. As in *The Turn of the Screw,* the "element of the unnamed and the untouched became . . . greater than any other." And as Foucault centrally observes in *La Volonté de savoir,* tracing the transformation of flesh into word in modern society, this refusal to name is not opposed to but part of the production and regulation of desire in discourse: "Silence itself—the things one declines to say, or is forbidden to name, the discretion that is required between different speakers—is less the absolute limit of discourse, the other side from which it is separated by a strict boundary, than an element that functions alongside the things said, with them and in relation to them within over-all strategies."[30] Jamesian discretion exemplifies this linking of silence and incitement.

The Jamesian text, we have seen, represents and displaces networks of power, knowledge, and desire. Again, these textual displacements produce what I have been calling the double discourse of the novel: power is displaced through a perpetual reference to something not itself, perpetually referred elsewhere and reappearing in areas ostensibly "entirely different" from the political.[31] The novel advertises an essential incompatibility between art and power, advertises indeed the freedom and autonomy of the aesthetic.

One version of this antinomy, and of the notion of autonomy that it supports, appears in the familiar Jamesian polarizing of an integral and autonomous self against what he, in *The Portrait of a Lady* (chapter 19), calls the self's "cluster of appurtenances" and "envelope of circumstances." In *The Ivory Tower* this polarity of self and society, or rather of interior and exterior determinations of the self, is almost diagrammatically represented in the contrast of Gray's "inward consumption" to the conspicuous consumption of America's "outward show" (pp. 74, 55). In *The*

---

30. Michel Foucault, *The History of Sexuality* (New York: Pantheon, 1980), 27.
31. Michel Foucault, *Discipline and Punish,* 22.

American Scene James noted the American "triumph of the superficial."[32] In *The Ivory Tower* he sets Gray against the money-passion and reign of appearance. Thus, if Horty Vint is seen to be "at the mercy of his appearance," Gray lays claim to a self-determination that controls what might be easily be called his publication: "My appearance," he asserts, despite his inheritance of a fortune, "would depend only on myself" (pp. 196, 207). But if Gray declares his independence from the money-power, the novel finally tells a different story. If James contraposes the ivory tower to "the black and merciless things that are behind the great possessions" (p. 295), this black-and-white polarity screens just the criminal continuity that Gray finally represents. The very notion of a free-floating and autonomous self (or text) reinvokes the very economy it would escape: as Gayatri Spivak notes in another context, "It is not too far from the truth to suggest that this freedom of choice by a freely choosing subject . . . is the ideology of free enterprise at work."[33] More particularly, and in line with the logic we have been tracing, James's techniques of representation in *The Ivory Tower* reinvent the technologies of power he disavows, and these techniques cover for the very power that literally sponsors, endows, and underwrites them.

If James rejects the American outward show, we have seen that his own "richly superficial" art is itself an art of appearance.[34] The appeal of an advertising aesthetic is always implicit in James's fictional practice. James's "treatment" of his subjects, for instance, is strikingly reproduced in what Rosanna Gaw, in *The Ivory Tower,* calls "an advertisement of all the latest knowledge of how to 'treat' every inch of the human surface" (p. 50). Referring to "Gray's appearance," Cissy declares, "What are

---

32. Henry James, *The American Scene* (Bloomington: Indiana University Press, 1968), 465.

33. Gayatri Chakravorty Spivak, "The Politics of Interpretations," *Critical Inquiry* 9 (September 1982), 264.

34. Leo Bersani makes a case for James's "richly superficial art" in *A Future for Astyanax* (Boston: Little, Brown, 1976), 128–55.

photographs, the wretched things, but the very truth of life?"
(pp. 173, 175). It is of course just such an art of appearance, just
such a claim about truth in advertising, that Gray refuses. He
rejects the power of show and, despite the wealth with which he
has been endowed, insists that "I don't in the least judge that I
am, or can at all be advertised as, one of the really big" (p. 206).

The insistence on an essential autonomy of self, and on the
autonomy of the "culture" that Gray represents, could not be
clearer. But Gray in fact cannot avoid becoming precisely the
image of what he disowns. His very refusal to become a mon-
eyed "monster on exhibition" turns out to be "*the* feature of the
scene" (p. 207). Gray simply enough becomes an *advertisement of
his difference:* the advertised alternative to the money-power, the
image of its opposite. More than that, he cannot avoid functioning as that power's "facade" and "front" (p. 206). And indeed it
is just this screening image of the opposite, his benefactor explains, that "our great public demands": "We require the difference that you'll make" (p. 112). What is required, and what is
produced, is the "difference" and alternative to power that
makes that power tolerable.

The ivory tower, screening within its secret compartment the
black secrets of the great possessions, perfectly emblematizes the
double discourse of power in the novel that we have been tracing: the ivory tower is the ruse of power. Finally, *The Ivory Tower*
recapitulates the displacements and suppressions of power, and
the comprehensive disavowal of the shame of power that define
the Jamesian text. It recapitulates as well the criminal continuity
between art and power that is the almost unreadable lesson of
the Jamesian novel. The power *of* the novel is that it masks the
power *in* the novel, even as the novel acts as a cover and relay of
that power.

Postscript

Reading Foucault:
Cells, Corridors, Novels

I

Jacques Donzelot ends his account of nineteenth-century social practices of discipline and regulation, *The Policing of Families*, with this little story:

> At Easter time in 1976, an obscure inmate of a provincial prison died as the result of a long hunger strike that he had embarked upon because, in his judicial dossier, only his faults, his deviations from the norm, his unhappy childhood, his marital instability, had been noted down, but not his endeavors, his searchings, the aleatory train of his life. It seems that this was the first time a prison hunger strike had ended in a death, the first time too that one had been undertaken for so bizarre a motive.[1]

This small narrative is interesting on several counts, not least because what this anonymous and marginal but well-documented—well-documented because marginal—figure seems to have resisted above all is his arrest as the subject of narrative

1. Jacques Donzelot, *The Policing of Families*, trans. Robert Hurley (New York: Pantheon, 1979), 234.

treatment. More precisely, he seems to have resisted the sort of narrative in which he has been inscribed. What has *not* been recorded are his searches and drifts—the aleatory career of the picaro. What *has* been recorded—marking a shift in the discourse of criminality—are the petty and malicious minutiae, the everyday delinquencies and abnormalities of family life and conjugality. The difference between these two stories is in fact a difference *about* difference. If the first links transgression and quest, the second registers a technology of power that operates "to assimilate the transgression of the laws into a general tactic of subjection."[2] "Instability," deviation, and difference appear not as the means of escaping power but as the points of that power's application. The subject, inhabiting a normative scenario that defines his "individuality" in the act of confiscating it as deviation, is produced at an exemplary crossing of knowledge, discourse, and power. Not surprisingly, his protest is situated at the place where these regulative technologies cross—the body. In the sense that I have earlier indicated, it might further be said that this story reads as a miniature and foreshortened version of the genre that so closely resembles the police report and judicial dossier—the realist novel—not merely in its detailed and "criminal" content but also in its form, the relentlessly coherent, determined, and "genetic" progress, always in a direction preestablished, from unhappy childhood to unhappy marriage to this twofold bringing to book.

Donzelot's close, however, hints also at a different and opposed sort of story, hints at a certain narrative reversal—an undramatic passion and resurrection of the body ("Easter time") and the initiation of a certain, barely defined resistance (for "the first time . . . too"). How are we to read this somewhat "too literary" reversal? And more generally, how are we to read this recalcitrant opposition of the literary and the political in a text that everywhere traces the comprehensive production and as-

---

2. Michel Foucault, *Discipline and Punish: The Birth of the Prison*, trans. Alan Sheridan (New York: Pantheon, 1977), 292. Subsequent references appear in parentheses in the text, preceded by *DP*.

similation of opposition and difference as a tactic of power? How should we read this difference—and the difference of the literary—in a text that centrally traces what might be called a reactionary "deployment of difference"?

The closing passage of Donzelot's explicitly Foucauldian history concisely poses the related matters that I have been addressing: first, the character of the social technologies that Foucault has been elaborating in his more recent work and the networks of knowledge, discourse, and power that support these technologies and produce the subject as the subject of power; second, the relation between these technologies and the content and techniques of literary narrative, particularly the realist and naturalist novel, which becomes prominent at the same time that these disciplinary practices take power; third, and perhaps most significant for our purposes in this chapter, the uncertain status of resistance, opposition, and marginality, the uncertain status of difference within a political regime that, as Foucault and Donzelot have traced, operates through the production and "management" of differences.

To pose the questions of "the literary" and "the political" together is also to open the question of resistance, in part, as we have seen, because of the nineteenth-century production of the category of "the literary" as an oppositional or counter-discourse. Such a conception operates to guarantee an absolute antinomy between the literary and what I have generally been calling "the political" domain. According to this view, the literary is essentially opposed to and outside the political. Whether this externality of the literary to the political is founded on an "irony intrinsic to the literary" that decenters and undoes structures of power, or on a "critical difference" that must be repressed in any (therefore necessarily illegitimate) exercise of power, or on an "arbitrariness of the sign" taken to entail the repressive arbitrariness of any enforcement of power and meaning (terms that tend toward synonymy in this account)—however this antinomy has been theoretically posited, all these accounts of an internal difference in the literary rely upon an opposing of repression and subversion, of containment and liberating difference. They all project an essential autonomy of the literary and an intrinsic opposition of literary resistance and social practices of regulation.

It is this scenario that I have been questioning. What I want to clarify here are the ways in which the insistence on literary difference may in fact function as part of and end up reaffirming the very structures of power that the literary (and literary theory) are imagined to subvert. Put simply, the problem with founding the autonomy or privileged externality of the literary to the political on an intrinsic irony or difference is that, as Foucault has been tracing, irony and difference are themselves crucial to the operation of modern arrangements of power. Modern power arrangements of discipline and normalization aspire to a "double discourse" of disavowal and reinscription. From this point of view, the assertion of literary autonomy or subversiveness appears not as an escape from power but rather as part of that power's deployment. To adapt Foucault's formulation, "the irony of this deployment is in having us believe that our 'liberation' is in balance."[3]

It should by now be clear that the terms by which the literary and the political are opposed invoke the terms of what Foucault has called the "repressive hypothesis." Foucault has argued that the view of power as essentially negative, imprisoning, and censoring covers for the "productiveness" of modern power relations. Not merely does the view of power as comprehensively repressive and silencing automatically align speech and discourse with the promise of liberation; more generally, as we have seen, the notion of power as a pure limit set on freedom has become, in our society, the form of its acceptability. What makes power tolerable is its limitation *as* limit. And what this collaterally involves is the projection of a domain outside of

---

3. Michel Foucault, *The History of Sexuality*, trans. Robert Hurley (New York: Pantheon, 1978), 159. Subsequent references appear in parentheses in the text, preceded by *HS*.

power—the difference and alternative to power or "world else-where"—that makes power tolerable.

Modern power arrangements thus require difference, not only because the very production of differences, abnormalities, and anomalies extends the field of "normalizing" operations, but also because the production of differences promises a haven, or escape, from power. As Hubert L. Dreyfus and Paul Rabinow note, in *Michel Foucault: Beyond Structuralism and Hermeneutics*, "the repressive hypothesis—the lynchpin of bio-power—rests on this assumption of externality and difference." The human sciences—and the discourse of aesthetics—invoke a "privileged externality" and assume that the "truths they uncover lie outside the sphere of power" and occupy a space "outside" the matrices of discipline and regulation. Crucially, then, the assumption of externality, difference, and autonomy may ultimately support the very power moves it would seem to oppose. Again, if power is essentially silencing and repressive, then discourse speaks the truth that liberates, and in this way the deployment of difference may ultimately collate with the deployment of power. As Dreyfus and Rabinow argue, regulation "masks itself by producing a discourse, seemingly opposed to it, but really part of a larger deployment of power."[4]

If Foucault has attempted to demonstrate the ways in which the "opposition" of subversion and repression supports, in a circular fashion, what it seems to resist, Karlis Racevskis's *Michel Foucault and the Subversion of Intellect*—as the title itself indicates—tends to remain within the logic of this opposition, and it will be useful to indicate some of the consequences of that logic. Racevskis sees Foucault's own strategy as "profoundly liberating in its effects" and successful at "dismantling the system of constraints . . . with which Western civilization has established the norms and limits of humanity." He views Foucault's approach as

---

4. Hubert L. Dreyfus and Paul Rabinow, *Michel Foucault: Beyond Structuralism and Hermeneutics* (Chicago: University of Chicago Press, 1982), 182, 180–81, 132.

"fundamentally subversive" in its revelation that "society is an inherently flawed and highly deficient process" that represses "much of what is beyond the reach of rational understanding and control."[5]

The imprecision in Racevskis's account reflects at least in part the difficulty of aligning Foucault's analytic with a subversive and "positive" program, a matter to which we must return. But the imprecision also proceeds from Racevskis's sketchy indication of shifts and trajectories in Foucault's project, from the history of madness to the history of sexuality. Racevskis tends to conflate different and at times rival positions, so that, for instance, the continuities and significant discontinuities between Foucault's problematic attempt to speak the silent "other" of madness and his more recent critiques of the function of the "alternative" remain largely unread. Whereas Foucault in his earlier work—in *The Order of Things,* for instance—represented the literary as an essentially transgressive counter-discourse, he more recently has viewed the literary, not as a privileged source of resistance to normalizing and regulative social practices, but rather as one among other disciplinary practices. The novel thus appears as one of those documents, by no means merely "documentary," that constitute and police the real and individualize the subject, inciting, as we have seen, a social and psychological "secrecy" that must be disclosed, classified, positioned within networks of power and knowledge. By this view, literature has no privileged status at all, although its claims to be oppositional, as we will see, function as part of a more general ideology of power.[6]

But such a desire to see literature as power's subversive other governs Racevskis's ready assimilation of Foucault's strategies to a debatable reading of the Lacanian categories of the Imaginary and the Symbolic. Racevskis insists that Foucault's "purpose is

5. Karlis Racevskis, *Michel Foucault and the Subversion of Intellect* (Ithaca: Cornell University Press, 1983), 15, 16, 20.

6. See John Rajchman, "Foucault, or the Ends of Modernism," *October,* 24 (Spring 1983), pp. 37–62.

comparable to Lacan's, since it also consists in showing that 'man is not an object, but a being in the process of realizing itself, something metaphysical,' that our humanity is not the image we construe of ourselves but something over which we have little control." But although something of an analogy can be drawn here, such a linking is generally misleading. For one thing, Racevskis simply elides Foucault's critiques of psychoanalytic discourse, ignores above all Foucault's reading of psychoanalysis as yet another of the technologies of confession by which the desires of the subject are "taken into account" and deployed in modern Western society. For another, Racevskis sees the categories of the Imaginary and the Symbolic not as two interdependent modes of *representation* but rather as moral and political categories that fit neatly into a hierarchical arrangement—the point is to be "for" the Symbolic and "against" the Imaginary, or as it appears in Racevskis's account, "for" difference and "against" the same.[7]

Put somewhat differently, Racevskis thinks of the Symbolic as "better" than the Imaginary because he reads the relation between these categories as a relation of subversion and repression, arguing that "psychoanalysis [and, by extension, any discursive practice] can redeem itself every time it works to subvert its own Imaginary procedures." Such a promise of redemption is achieved, for Racevskis, through a heightened awareness of difference or, more basically, through an increase in "self-awareness." Thus the "very awareness" of paradox, contradiction, and difference is seen to give Foucault's strategy "its subversive potential." In all, Foucault, "acutely aware of his subjectivity," liberates a "new kind of awareness" and produces for the reader "an increased sense of self-consciousness" that is, again, "profoundly liberating in its effects."[8]

Interestingly enough, this liberating awareness is primarily an awareness of limits, a self-awareness of the grids of power and knowledge that traverse and inscribe the "self." There is per-

---

7. Racevskis, *Michel Foucault and the Subversion of Intellect*, 38.
8. Ibid., 51, 116, 30.

haps nothing unfamiliar about such an implicitly paradoxical logic—the logic of "I may be trapped, but at least I know it"— nor about the way in which the acknowledgment of limitation, though an internal torsion, becomes an escape from those limits. This double logic is a version of what Foucault has described as the "analytic of finitude" which, he argues in *The Order of Things*, has formed the (contradictory) basis of positive knowledge from Kant onward. In brief, such an analytic converts the subject's limitation by social and positive law into a principle of knowledge, and the awareness of these laws become "the right, through an interplay of these very laws, to know them and to subject them to a total clarification."[9] As Dreyfus and Rabinow suggest, the contortions of such a perspective promise "the possibility of turning the knower's messy involvement in the factual world of language, life, and labor into the pure ground of knowledge."[10] This contradiction also underwrites the "conventionalist" position in contemporary literary theory, a position that acknowledges the contextual and conventional constitution of knowledge and belief but does so only by implicitly positing an unconstrained position from which one might "choose" or "stand outside" context and beliefs. That is, the very acknowledgment that there is no escaping the constitutive force of contexts and beliefs is converted into a position of exemption from which one may assess the conventions and beliefs of others (or, effectively, of oneself as another); and what this contradiction elides is the unending (impossible) effort that would be involved in attempting to reappropriate one's own position and beliefs.

Clearly, a privileging self-reflexivity has been taken to define the literary difference; notions of the self-referential, self-conscious, and self-deconstructing character of the literary have formed a part of what Foucault has called "the whole relentless theorization of writing" and the more local theorization of the

9. Michel Foucault, *The Order of Things* (New York: Vintage, 1973), 310.
10. Dreyfus and Rabinow, *Michel Foucault*, 32.

literary as intrinsically oppositional.[11] For now it is necessary to note that both the "repressive hypothesis" and the "analytic of finitude," on different levels, work to assimilate opposition, tension, irony, paradox, and contradiction to a principle of knowledge and a scheme of liberation. Foucault's work, however, involves a rereading of these "figures" and outlines a rhetoric of power that points to another way of seeing these deployments of difference. Modern power relations, for Foucault, tell two apparently separate but in fact inseparable stories. The two-sidedness is in part a relation of masking: hence Foucault observes that "power is tolerable only on condition that it mask a substantial part of itself" (*HS*, p. 86). But this two-sidedness is also and more significantly a function of the double and "circular" logic of normalizing structures of power.

From one point of view, as we have seen, it is the divided nature of the norm—as that which simply is and as that which must be achieved—that immanently promotes a movement of normalization; from another, it is the production of gaps and contradictions that secures this movement. As I indicated in my account of *The Golden Bowl*, this is the structure of difference that Jacques Donzelot has described as a "system of flotation," as a system by which two apparently opposed structures are suspended in relation to each other, intrinsically promoting a coordination and adjustment of structures while protecting the differences that "oppose" these structures. Thus, Donzelot argues, Keynesian economics "adjusts" the social and economic spheres, at once maintaining the required autonomy of these spheres—of private enterprise and social welfare—and avoiding the "alternative of anarchic liberalism or authoritarian centralism." The "contradiction" between free enterprise and social welfare is, in principle, converted into a "circular functionality between the

---

11. Michel Foucault, "Truth and Power," trans. Colin Gordon, in *Power/Knowledge* (New York: Pantheon, 1980), 127, as cited in Rajchman, "Foucault, or the Ends of Modernism," 37. Rajchman traces Foucault's earlier participation in and later criticism of this relentless theorization.

two registers of the production of goods and the production of producers (and consumers)."

Similarly, Freud, according to Donzelot, provides a flexible mechanism of adjustment between the juridical and medical spheres that defends against, on the one hand, statist control of the family and, on the other hand, the danger of the family's autonomy. This tactically polyvalent and uneven development "facilitat[es] social regulation by referring the frustrations of individuals to the family," that is, to the family thoroughly injected with social norms of health and education. Put simply, the family is left "free" to police and justify itself, autonomous so long as it regulates itself. Donzelot suggests that Freud and Keynes together provide the model for a social mechanism that deploys contradiction and difference within a system of flotation that equilibrates "autonomy" and "regulation" while saving these categories and the saving contradiction between them.[12]

In both instances, the "liberal" differences between private initiative and social welfare, between possessive individualism and public norms, between, in all, private and public domains, are scrupulously preserved; at the same time, the "floating" of the categories in relation to each other provides them with a "principle of conversion" into one another. As Michael Ignatieff has suggested, advanced liberal society operates through a perpetual "adjudication of the claims of liberty and the claims of order."[13] Robin Evans, in *The Fabrication of Virtue*, his recent study of English prison and urban architecture of the eighteenth and nineteenth centuries, describes a similar coordination and management of public and private spaces, at once a segregation and marriage of social and individual imperatives. Discussing the Pennsylvania penitentiary system of cellular confinement, Evans notes that "in terms of planning, the separate prisons were comprised of a marriage between the static, shrouded, contemplative, individualized space of the cells and the generalized connective

---

12. Donzelot, *The Policing of Families*, 217–33.
13. Michael Ignatieff, *A Just Measure of Pain* (New York: Pantheon, 1978), 214.

space of the galleries converging on the central observatory." He adds that this marriage "between open and closed space was echoed more directly in housing than in factories, and this is not the only connection between prisons and housing." Indeed, the difference between private occupied space and public servicing space is duplicated within the model tenements, which were in fact advertised as a sort of *sanctuary* from a general public criminality. And since, as Evans shows, the difference between private and public spaces is mapped onto a difference between a private sphere of morality and goodness and a public sphere of promiscuous contagion and violent gregariousness and interpenetration, the tenement paradoxically duplicates the prison house in its very retreat from the evils of the social domain. It is again the contradictory segregation and connection of public and private, repeated on every level, that we find here, the necessity of a simultaneous protection and violation of differences, the simultaneous partitioning and interpenetration of spaces within the same "structure."[14]

In my treatments of *The Princess Casamassima* and the Philadelphia section of *The American Scene*, I have tried to map such a fantasmatics of confinement and contagion, of private retreats and enclosures and public exposure. Perhaps the richest novelistic representation of this architecture of regulation occurs in Zola's *L'Assommoir*. The tenement that centers the novel, and appears as a metonym of the city, is no longer Balzac's rooming house but rather a complexly interrelated and partitioned "block" of private and public spaces, of cells and corridors. In fact, Zola's mapping of spaces and of the circulation of populations explicitly reproduces on the narrative level the reordering, the opening and segregation, of urban space, achieved by Baron Haussmann, the "artist in demolition" who reconfigured Paris; and this reordering regulates the chronology of the novel.

The tenement is at once "barracks," "prison," and "factory,"

---

14. Robin Evans, *The Fabrication of Virtue* (Cambridge: Cambridge University Press, 1982), 404–19.

one of the new institutions of the disciplinary society in which an economy of discipline inheres in the architectural arrangements themselves. The proper circulation in the world of the novel is between the private space of the family and the public space of work, a "going constantly to and fro between home" and workplace. The bars that occupy the barriers or margins (at the walls and octroi) between the two domains divert and block this circulation between home and shop. And if the disjoining of the two sites leads to the "inevitable downfall" of the working-class family, their absolute identification—the cohabitation of public and private, as in Gervaise's laundry-home—equally produces a "loosening" of moral and familial ties.

The workplace in Zola's novel is an arena at once of eroticism and discipline, and this double discourse, this discipline of desire, breaks down when public and private spaces infiltrate and violate each other. What is required, as we have seen, is a simultaneous linking and segregation of domains. What violates this normative principle is a promiscuous mixing, on one side, or withdrawal, on the other. Gervaise's taking of her former lover into the home, without securing the dividing wall, over-"extends" the family ("the walls must surely fall down"), as her daughter's conversion of her bedroom into a sort of "open" house, in *Nana*, allows the street to infect the home. And Gervaise's final and deadly locus, neither in the private space of the apartment nor on the street but rather in the tenement corridor, emblematizes the final dissolution of the regulative movement that traces the normative grid of the novel. In the play of cell and corridor we read the perpetual adjustments of public and private domains "floated" in relation to each other.

Foucault has argued that such a system of flotation governs the representation of modern power arrangements. On one level, there is the "official" representation of power—as sovereignty and legal codes and apparatuses; on another, the barely visible, tiny and meticulous disciplines of everyday life. Although there is a constant functional interchange between the two levels, Foucault insists that "they cannot possibly be reduced to each other. The powers of modern society are exercised through, on the basis of, and by virtue of, this very heterogeneity between a public right of sovereignty and a polymorphous disciplinary mechanism."[15] The strategic irreducibility or disarticulation of these representations thus provides the linchpin of modern political technologies. As Foucault suggests, "the general juridical form that guaranteed a system of rights that were egalitarian in principle was supported by these tiny, everyday, physical mechanisms, by all those systems of micro-power that are essentially non-egalitarian and asymmetrical that we call disciplines" (*DP*, p. 222). Racevskis notes that the two forms of representation seem to be at odds but in fact coexist and reinforce each other; if their relation seems paradoxical, Racevskis notes, "this paradox does not therefore constitute a contradiction from the point of view of an effective social arrangement."[16]

Or rather, this paradox constitutes a contradiction that is precisely effective. Foucault describes this contradiction as a strategic opposition of form and content, commenting that the purpose of panoptic and normalizing arrangements of power is "to make the effective mechanisms of power function in opposition to the formal framework that it had acquired" (*DP*, p. 222). The double discourse of power thus requires a strategic opposition and difference—an aporetic moment; it requires a power of separation and a separation of powers in order to operate. Difference is required to project an "alternative" and privileged externality to regulative mechanisms, even as this difference establishes the relational equilibrium or system of flotation that correlates "autonomy" and "regulation."

II

The notion of the privileged externality of discourse, and more narrowly, of the autonomy of the literary, might be understood

---

15. Michel Foucault, "Two Lectures," in *Power/Knowledge*, 106.
16. Racevskis, *Michel Foucault and the Subversion of Intellect*, 101.

in terms of such a system of flotation. It is not hard to see that the recalcitrant oppositions of history and textuality, power and discourse, politics and aesthetics, maintain an "insoluble" problem—the mutual exteriority of discursive and nondiscursive practices. Shifting the terms of this problem about, we might ask not "how resolve this problem of difference?" but rather "what problem does this difference solve?" On the model of Keynes and Freud, we might say that two questions have been implicitly posed in contemporary theory: "how protect the autonomy of the literary without sacrificing its worldliness?" and "how defend worldliness from the abyss of textuality?" Put somewhat differently, "how maintain textuality as a haven from power while avoiding the danger of an irresponsible anarchy or—in E. D. Hirsch's evocative phrase—'cognitive atheism'?" That is, "how maintain a zone free of power that is nonetheless regulated by 'normal' ('communal' or 'universal') values and significances?" Or yet again, "how maintain the view of the literary, and particularly of the novel, as at once in the world but not of it?"

Theoretical answers to these questions repress the circular functionality of these "opposed" terms, converting a tautology into an opposition that must constantly be renegotiated. Specialists in undecidability endlessly shuttle between cells and corridors in a theoretical and aesthetic duplication of the double discourse of power. The categories (and values) of irony, ambiguity, paradox, aporia, and contradiction have been deployed—in formalist, deconstructionist, and Marxist criticism—to "exempt" the literary, or to mark its internal difference, from the political. But these theorizings of a necessary incompatibility between worldly and textual functions (between the political and the literary, between rhetoric and grammar, between history and discourse, and so forth) inhabit the structure from which they would seem to exit. The "literary" contradiction between autonomy and regulation (between "liberation" and "repression") has the circular efficiency of the normalizing operation. The very instability and oscillation between the terms of the double reading deploy the power such a reading seems to deplore. This exit from power is a revolving door.

The double discourse of the realist novel has been read, both in traditional and in deconstructionist criticism, as an inherent tension or ambivalence within the novel. Thus, George Levine, in his recent *The Realistic Imagination,* speaks of "the self-contradictory nature of realism itself." Levine sees the self-contradiction in terms of a certain struggle within the novel: the realist novel displays "admirable struggles to get at truth without imprisoning it in conventions." Correlatively, the realist novel, on the side of a liberating "truth" and against "imprisoning" forms and conventions, centrally displays a tension between the imperatives of subject and the imperatives of treatment. "The continuing literary problem that plagued realism from the start," Levine observes, "was the incompatibility of tight form with plausibility." And Levine assents to Northrop Frye's assertion that "the realistic writer soon finds that the requirements of literary form and plausible content always fight against each other."[17]

The deconstructive practice of double reading rewrites these contradictions as an intrinsic literary "difference," or more specifically, Jonathan Culler observes, as a "structure of undecidability" produced by the "convergence of two narrative logics that do not give rise to a synthesis." Culler identifies the two incompatible logics as "story" and "discourse"—as, respectively, the events that must be conceived of as "independent" of any particular narrative presentation and "the force of meaning" and "demands of narrative coherence" that contradict this independence. Narrative thus displays a paradoxical economy by which, for instance, a character's actions are seen at once as the cause of consequent events and as the effect of narrative demands, as at once independent of and constrained by the force of the narrative system; "free choice" and systemic constraints are floated in relation to each other, never quite coordinated, at once insep-

---

17. George Levine, *The Realistic Imagination: English Fiction from Frankenstein to Lady Chatterley* (Chicago: University of Chicago Press, 1981), 7, 11.

arable and never quite capable of harmonious synthesis. In his earlier *Structuralist Poetics,* Culler had defined a somewhat similar narrative paradox, "that fundamental tautology of fiction which allows us to infer character from action and then to be pleased at the way in which action accords with character." The logic of double reading converts this "tautology" into an absolute incompatibility, converts an oscillation between autonomy and regulation within a single structure into a principle of undecidability. But it is just the *tautological* structure of the double discourse of power that I have tried to indicate, and just this separation of the "moments" of the tautology into distinct and irreconcilable differences that secures at once the theoretical project and the aesthetic and theoretical rewriting of power. The irony of this rewriting is that it underwrites, on the level of theory (or *as* theory) the very arrangements of power it disowns. The absolute incompatibility of narrative logics, Culler insists, produces the "force of the narrative" and the text's "intriguing and dislocatory power." But this power of the novel might be seen somewhat differently. Concluding his account of the divided logic of narrative, Culler observes that "one must be willing to shift from one perspective to the other," one must be willing, that is, to "oscillate" from story (acts and choices) to discourse (the system of narrative) and back again. What I want to suggest is that the willingness to submit to the double logic of narrative is also a willingness to inhabit a certain style of power. And it is perhaps this submission that the discourse of the novel, both as a form and as an institution, has most comprehensively operated to achieve.[18]

Shifting the emphasis somewhat, we might say that narrative fiction plays out, in exemplary fashion, a certain anxiety about "how language relates to the world," a certain anxiety about "representation." In the terms that Richard Rorty has provided,

---

18. Jonathan Culler, *The Pursuit of Signs: Semiotics, Literature, Deconstruction* (Ithaca: Cornell University Press, 1981), 169–87; *Structuralist Poetics: Structuralism, Linguistics, and the Study of Literature* (Ithaca: Cornell University Press, 1975), 143.

we might see this anxiety as part of an "attempt to 'ground' predicative discourse on a nonconventional relation to reality." One consequence of the attempt, according to Rorty, has been the theorizing of distinctions between "real world talk" and "fictional discourse," between responsible and "first-rate discourse" (reports on what's out there) and irresponsible and "second-rate discourse" (making things up). Such distinctions promise "an account of our representations of the world which guarantees that we have not lost touch with it." We might say that, from a traditional perspective, the problem has been to enforce a difference between being "really out there" and being "made up" in order to guarantee the "tie" between language and world, and, from a deconstructionist perspective, to enforce the difference to guarantee the absence of such a tie and hence the inherent indeterminacy of meaning.[19]

But as Rorty implies, both perspectives depend upon a representational account of discourse that is basically mistaken. "The common root of all these problems," Rorty argues, "is the fear [or promise] that the manifold possibilities offered by discursive thought will play us false, will make us 'lose contact' with the real."[20] Put somewhat differently, the root of these problems is a division between discourse and world and a consequent tension between an irresponsible or autonomous discourse and a discourse regulated by its "tie" to the world. Such a position remains committed to a divided and contradictory account of the true: to a disinterested truth (that stands outside mere belief) and to an interested belief (that cannot guarantee its contact with truth). The need to protect a division between real world talk and fictional discourse is thus part of a desire to protect a distinction between truth and mere convention, between knowledge, on one side, and mere beliefs and interests, on the other—just the distinctions that the pragmatist account centrally con-

---

19. Richard Rorty, "Is There a Problem about Fictional Discourse?" in *Consequences of Pragmatism (Essays 1972–1980)* (Minneapolis: University of Minnesota Press, 1982), 130, 129.

20. Ibid., 130.

tests. The need is thus to guarantee a "contact" (or gap) between discourse and world. In the pragmatist view that Rorty presents, just this representational concept of discourse, in its "positive" or in its "negative" form, produces a problem about the status of fictional discourse and the need to theorize a distinction between worldly and fictional discourse. But if, in this pragmatist view, there is finally "no problem about fictional discourse," we might still ask why the problem has been reproduced and maintained within the realist novel, as a problem both in the novel (in the struggle between form and content) and of the novel (in the question of the novel's relation to the world). What ideological and institutional benefits might accrue in maintaining this problem as the problematic of the novel?

We have already seen that the perpetual coordinations and readjustments of subject and treatment in the Jamesian text— for instance, the advertised incompatibility between political subject and nonpolitical technique, between surveillance and novelistic ways of seeing in *The Princess Casamassima,* the coordination of "their fortune and my own method" in *The Golden Bowl*—register the double discourse of the Jamesian novel. The contradictory requirements of subject and treatment, far from putting the novel's regulative power in jeopardy, secure that power, or rather secure it precisely by insisting on its insecurity. Such a paradoxical movement, we have seen, may operate to support the double discourse of the realist novel. We have already traced the deployment of a difference between public and domestic spaces, between corridor and cell, in Zola's *L'Assommoir.* A similar tension defines the practice *of* the novel as well. In his preface to *L'Assommoir,* Zola offers two not entirely compatible "defenses" of the novel. On one side, the novel is defended in terms of its detailed realism: as an accurate depiction of "the polluted atmosphere of our urban areas," it is "a work of truth, the first novel about the common people which does not tell lies but has the authentic smell of the people." But on the other, the novel is exculpated in terms of a formal purity that explicitly resists the contamination of its "filthy" subject matter. If the author has been "accused of every kind of crime," he responds, "Form! Form is the great crime," and adds that his aim in the novel was "to do a purely philological study." Yet if Zola fails to notice the incompatibility of these defenses, perhaps he does so because this "tension" between form and subject functions for the novel as well as within it. These contradictory defenses—the defense of realism and the defense of formalism—are not finally at odds in the naturalist novel. As we have seen, it is the inevitable, formal "progress" and "logic" of the naturalist novel that *polices the real* and imposes what is literally a politics of form on the criminal content of the novel. If the naturalist novel appears at once as criminal and as a policing action, if Zola appears at once as a "drinker of blood" and as a "dull bourgeois" ("If they only knew what a dull bourgeois this drinker of blood, this ferocious novelist is"), this indicates not the internal contradictions that "undo" the naturalist project but rather the contradictions that constitute and maintain the double discourse of the novel.

I am suggesting, then, that the power *in* the novel and the power *of* the novel may be furthered by the very tensions and insecurities that split the practice of the novel. In his recent *Factual Fictions: Origins of the English Novel*, Lennard J. Davis traces the "constitutively-ambivalent" practice of the early English novel, the ways in which the novel is divided in its commitments, at once, to "reports on the world" and fictional invention, to "fact and fiction, news and novels, reportage and invention." Davis concludes by broaching the possibility that "in the disjunction and dialectic between these apparent contraries rests the foundation for the power of the novel in society and in the bourgeois imagination."[21] Although this connection between novelistic disjunction and bourgeois ideology remains somewhat provisional in Davis's study, and although his subject is the seventeenth- and eighteenth-century novel, the ambivalences he maps in the early novel can perhaps take us a step further in considering the double discourse of the realist novel.

21. Lennard J. Davis, *Factual Fictions: Origins of the English Novel* (New York: Columbia University Press, 1983), 211.

Davis argues that the crucial ambivalence in the novel between factual and fictional imperatives produces a paradoxical "phenomenology of reading" such that the reader, experiencing the novel at once as a "report on the world" and as a "framed" world elsewhere, must "split his perception" of the text consumed. The reader must in effect be in two places at once. If the reader is "brought within the frame of the discourse both spatially and temporally," he is paradoxically also made "more a part of that world" that the novel brings news of. What Davis calls the "news/novels" matrix puts the reader in motion between these two insistently segregated but also communicating domains. What is effected is not merely an ambivalent exchange between the private world of reading and the public world of news but also a publication of the private and domestic, and a privatization of the social. Extending the terms of Davis's argument, we might say that if the novel "allow[s] history to enter the non-public realm," it also allows the private realm to enter history. In this "private" consumption of the public and "public" documentation of the private, the novel supports both the documentary production of the "subject" that Foucault reads as a crucial achievement of the disciplinary society and, more generally, the ideological "system of flotation" that we have been sketching.[22]

For Davis, the tension between news and novel above all makes for the productive insecurity of the novel, as a form and as an institution. A different but not unrelated tension exists in the traditional novel of the nineteenth century. The history of the later nineteenth-century novel is in part a history of the redefinition of the terrain of the "novelistic" in relation to the rival, or alternatively, corroborative, discourses of journalism, sociology, and other reports on the world. The mid and later nineteenth-century novel's attempt to locate a "middle ground" between realist and romance imperatives may be read as an attempt to locate a point of intersection between fictional and real world commitments—a point of intersection that nonethe-

---

22. Ibid., 74, 114.

less retains the ratifying differences between social and individual domains and between the world "out there" and the fictional "world elsewhere." Perhaps the clearest example of this divided and dividing practice is the work of Hawthorne, whose fiction attempts both to "open an intercourse with the world" and to protect a private space of romance. And perhaps the most concise instance of the "disjunction and dialectic" in Hawthorne's fiction occurs in the scene (chapter 17) in *The House of the Seven Gables* in which Clifford and Hepzibah take flight from the seclusion of their ancestral house into what Hawthorne calls "the world."

The railway car that transports the fugitives is something of a mobile home or halfway house, located between the "stale ideas of home and fireside" they have fled and the "rapid current of affairs" they are entering. The "interior life" of the train that "had taken their two selves into its grasp" is at once a public and a domestic space, housing "fifty human beings in close relation with them, under one long and narrow roof." Not merely does the train represent a juncture between public and private sites, but also its "to-and-fro" movement is a movement—literally, a commuting—between home and marketplace. Above all, and not finally unlike the regulative movement we have sketched in Zola, the train traces a movement between dangerously opposed fixations: on one side, an absolute domestic withdrawal ("This one old house was everywhere!"), at the other, the complete immersion of self in the marketplace (the danger that "the market should ravish them away"). The attempt is to locate a point of intersection between home and marketplace, an intercourse emblematically represented, of course, by the opening of the shop door in the house of the seven gables.

What must be emphasized here, however, is the way in which the novel itself participates in the movement it represents. For one thing, the interior life of the railway car is also a space of reading, and of reading precisely regulated to the "commuting" of the readers: "Some, with tickets in their hats, long travellers these, before whom lay a hundred miles of railroad, had plunged into the English scenery and adventures of pamphlet novels. . . . Others, whose briefer span forbade their devoting themselves to studies so abstruse, beguiled the tedium of the way with penny-papers." News and novels supply a shorter or longer movement between the reader's private space and the world; the market productions of news and novels transport and "beguile" the reader doubly shuttling between home and marketplace. The novel is thus both for commuters and a commuter itself, representing and enacting an exchange between domesticity and the marketplace of the world. Nor is this commuter literature merely a "sham" commercial production. For if *The Scarlet Letter* opens by putting Hester Prynne—the scarlet letter herself—on display in the "Market-Place," and if *The House of the Seven Gables* promotes the opening of the house to the shop, these novels at once resist and enact a necessary "exchange" between romance and novel, privacy and publication, fiction and market. The mid-century romance retains a critical and "oppositional" character in its very resistances to what Hawthorne calls the requirements of "the novel," retains its oppositional force, we might say, even as it points to the conversion of oppositions into the regulative management of crises and differences that, I have been arguing, defines the late nineteenth-century novel.

III

Such an account points both to the immanence of power *in* the novel and to the power *of* the novel: the manner in which the novel at once acts as a relay of social mechanisms of regulation and lays claim to an autonomy and difference from the political, a claim to autonomy that may ultimately support these mechanisms. Such an arrangement relies on instabilities and paradoxes in order to function: the "corporate" novel of the late nineteenth-century specializes in crisis management. Again, I am not saying that instabilities are automatically or even in principle recuperable, merely "decoy" productions. But I am saying that there is a fundamental problem with a critical discourse that founds the "privilege" of the literary—its difference from the political—on its paradoxical, contradictory, or intrinsically self-deconstructing forms. The politics of the novel, and problems of resistance and recuperation, are not theoretical matters, although one might attempt, as I have, to map a politics of theory. Rather, these problems are located on a more "trivial," ordinary, and heterogeneous level, the level that the novel, for instance, takes as its domain.

But the figure of the *tautology* that I have invoked may be somewhat misleading here. If this figure implicitly governs, as I have argued, the double discourse of the Jamesian text and of the late nineteenth-century novel generally, it suggests what might be called a "formalization" or "totalization" of power-discourse relations in the novel. The double discourse of the Jamesian novel perhaps provides the ideal form of a specific regime of regulation, as Bentham's Panopticon provides the ideal form of a specific technology of discipline. But Bentham's model was never—never totally—constructed, and if social practices and discourses of discipline and normalization aspire to the circular efficiency of a zero-sum model of power, such an absolute "coding" of power relations is a theoretical fiction.

Foucault has emphasized how even the "weak links" in the multiple and heterogeneous apparatuses of power may become usable for those apparatuses, how "all those things which 'don't work'" can "ultimately serve to make the thing 'work.'"[23] But although Foucault is routinely criticized for an overly monolithic conception of power, he in fact insists on the local and unstable moves of often conflicting apparatuses of discipline, administration, and regulation, localizations and instabilities that define at once the field of regulative practices and the limits on and resistances to those practices. If, as Foucault maintains, resistance

---

23. Michel Foucault, *Le Monde*, October 21, 1978, as cited in Colin Gordon, "Afterword," *Power/Knowledge*, 257.

is not "outside" power, neither is resistance always already conscripted or preempted. Rather, as Dreyfus and Rabinow note, "Resistance is both an element in the functioning of power and a source of its perpetual disorder."[24]

The "instability" of power thus cuts both ways, though it does not reduce to an "ambiguity" or undecidability about historically specific relations of power and resistance. The realist and naturalist novel aspires to a "totalizing" conscription of differences within systems of regulation, aspires to convert even what escapes it into points of support. But instruments of power may be reappropriated, and lines of force reversed. "Turning the tables," as we saw in *The Golden Bowl*, is always a possibility. In fact, we have seen that the notion of a binary division between power and resistance—the desire for an "outside" to power—idealizes arrangements of power in the very gesture of disowning them. If I have been emphasizing the way in which the novel can operate as a relay of regulative and disciplinary practices, this is in part because, as I have tried to show, the assumption that the novel, necessarily and in principle, provides a haven or escape from power has become one of the ideological supports of that power. More specifically, if Henry James's work has been appropriated to support an essential difference between the art of the novel and the subject of power, that work provides a virtual map of disciplinary and regulative practices, not least in its claims to stand outside and to oppose those practices.

Foucault has cautioned against a "theoretical totalization under the guise of 'truth'"; it is necessary as well to defend against a theoretical totalization under the guise of "power."[25] At one extreme, it is necessary to avoid a "literary" reading of difference and contradiction as a necessary "undoing" of power; at the other, to avoid a totalizing reading of power as a necessarily preemptive regulation of difference; at both, to avoid reducing

24. Dreyfus and Rabinow, *Michel Foucault*, 147.
25. Michel Foucault, "Intellectuals and Power," in *Language, Counter-Memory, Practice: Selected Essays and Interviews*, ed. Donald F. Bouchard (Ithaca: Cornell University Press, 1977), 217.

the double discourse of power to a theoretical model of ambiguity or undecidability. I have tried to revise the governing view of power in and of the later nineteenth-century novel by providing an account of the microhistories and micropolitics that traverse the discourse of the novel. Such an account is necessarily partial, local, and provisional, a history of novels rather than a theory of "the Novel." My attempt has been to provide a historically specific "opening" to a reconsideration of the politics of the novel, a reconsideration that might begin here.

Index